Not So Long Ago

B N Tandan

Dedication

This book is dedicated to all who are interested in history, ancient or modern.

Acknowledgments

This book took two years to write, as I had to check some facts with my sister Sidya Bahen and kept trying to keep it from becoming too voluminous, as the time period written about is vast. Some memories were revived as I was writing, and some were deleted for brevity.

If my recollections are different from some of my contemporaries, I beg forgiveness for my perception of events and facts as I remember them. If it rekindles some of their memories, then my efforts would not have been in vain.

I thank my wife, Ursula, for having been patient with me as I spent quite a bit of time alone in writing this.

Biren Tandan. Hammonton, N.J., U.S.A.

About the Author

Dr. Tandan was born in Agra, India, trained in and practiced Urologic Surgery in the U.S. for 50 yrs. and lives there. He is a Diplomate of the American Board of Urology. Fellow of the American College of Surgeons, Fellow of the International College of Surgeons Member of the Indian Academy of Medical Sciences (Surgery). Lt. Col. (Rtd) U.S.A.F- R, and belongs to many other medical and social organizations.

PREFACE

This is not a memoir in the true sense. It is a compilation of my memories and the times strung on the thread of my early life. I see the world changing rapidly, much more than when I was a child. I also detect a tendency to lack interest in the past and to learn from it. Which, as the old adage says, can be detrimental. The rapidity of change and the faster pace of life leaves little time to reminisce and recount the past. This lack of interest in History as a whole, even in comparatively recent events, as not worthy of our time and efforts is regrettable. Not only can we learn from it and try to avoid mistakes of the past, but we also understand it, wonder at it, and rejoice in its triumphs and glory. We can also see where and how we were and how it has shaped the present.

Why would the reader want to read about India and its recent past? It is to see how a country changed from a brutal colonial past of over 150 yrs, then dismemberment and disruption, and has transformed into the world's fifth largest economy in a span of less than 70yrs, remained a stable democracy, while all around it countries imploded into chaos and dictatorships. It went from frequent famines to a top exporter of agricultural products, pharmaceuticals, vaccines and other goods and has the largest film industry in the world. Produced a nuclear deterrent, space satellites, a rover to Mars and a successful moon landing- all within 70 yrs of Independence. Its diaspora, forcibly sent as indentured laborers to West Indies, Guyana, Suriname, Fiji, Mauritius, East Africa, are Presidents and Prime ministers there. The prime minister of the U.K. (Rishi Sunak), Irish republic (Varadkar) cabinet ministers in Canada, two state governors in the US (Nikki Haley and Bobby Jindal) and the Vice President of the US (Kamala Harris are of Indian origin. The CEOs of Novartis, Starbucks, Microsoft, Google and other corporations are Indians. Indians have won 9 Nobel prizes. But in most people's eyes it is still a 'Third world' country. So it is important to know what was before all this.

Recalling the past is like exploring an old attic. You come across things that bring back fond memories, wonderment, and surprises, joyous and sometimes sad. It is not always accurate, but it is uniquely ours. Sometimes faded, dim and dusty, and sometimes as real as now. I have described the places where I grew up in detail, for they have either disappeared and are hard to imagine or have been modified beyond recognition.

I have used American English since most of my life has been spent in the U.S., and that is how I think and speak now.

I have also used the spelling 'Tandon' for the surname of my Indian family, as that is how it is overwhelmingly spelled in India. For some reason, my father used 'Tandan,' which my sons and I have followed.

This is a collection of my memories of the times gone by as I saw and now remember them. So take a moment and dive deep into another world- the past, with me.

Old age is not all it is cracked up to be. But to attain it with a reasonable modicum of physical and mental health is in itself an achievement. Having achieved it with some luck and reconciled to the diminution of physical and mental faculties, one becomes a bit philosophic and introspective. What have I accomplished? Did it have any meaning? Did I make any difference? Was it all for nothing? These and many such questions arise. And have risen in people's minds since time immemorial, and will arise, hopefully, far into the future. Similar thoughts rose in my mind too.

Not being blessed with the fortune to leave an indelible mark, or even a modest one, got me thinking. The tides of Time erase the past at a much faster rate than its waves did in the distant past, and things are replaced, forgotten, or obliterated with bewildering speed- or so it seems. "What a waste! What a shame!" The old mind laments. Then a weak voice from within whispers, "Give it a try. Sketch a portrait of your journey and try to recount it to your younger near and dear ones and hopefully others so they can get some idea of real life in the past instead of from movies and such. To the survivors of my generation, to help them reminisce before it all gets washed away by Time."

The irony is that people show great curiosity, go to great lengths to research, excavate and speculate the distant, ancient past and ignore or forget the recent one. So, readers, this is a feeble attempt to recollect the times, events, and people in my life as I look back with wonder. It is neither complete nor objective and may differ from the recollections of my dwindling contemporaries. I sincerely hope to enable you to take a glimpse of the past through the retro-scope of my memory to what was- the good, the bad, and the ugly.

Consider this a garland of the blossoms my mind picked and threaded through the string of my life. Whether it refreshes your mind with the faint and wispy aroma of the past or not, I offer it to you with humility and hope.

The Beginning

I was born on the afternoon of the birth anniversary of the poet Tulsidas, at the Thompson Hospital in Agra, in the year 1938. I was the fifth born and the first male child of my parents. Male offspring were of great importance in a Hindu family, not only to carry on the family name but also for religious reasons. My grandfather (Baba) had waited at the hospital for my mother to deliver after she went into labor early that morning, but left in disgust just before I was born, supposedly remarking that it was no use waiting as she would have a girl anyway, just as before. So I was a surprise, at least to my grandpa, hopefully, a pleasant one. I never had the nerve to ask. No other details were mentioned except that I was plump like other male newborns in the family.

My first memory, strangely, is of my mother banging my head against an iron railing as I screamed. My father came up and took me away and consoled me on his lap. I don't know how old I was or what happened to incite her rage, but my mother never yelled or laid a hand on me since and was the gentlest person I have ever known. It was also the first and last time I experienced any open expression of affection from my dad. My immediate sibling was my sister Sidya Bahen, more than eight years my senior. My mother had lost one female offspring post-partum. Another child died of unknown causes in early childhood. Her name was Rajni. She was rarely mentioned, except by my mother, in her later years. When the topic would come up, my mother's eyes would moisten, and she would say wistfully that she was a beautiful girl.

I grew up in the inner city in one of the most efficiently designed compact houses I have ever known, which my father rented. I will take the liberty to elaborate. It was at the corner of the main lane and a side one with entrances at each. The front entrance was a step above the lane into the living room. To the right was a tiny room, my father's office, and to the left, another room with a door and two small windows to the front. It had a wide wooden bed (Takht) and was used as a male guest bedroom. A door in the back of the living room opened into a narrow courtyard with an open stairway against the back wall going to the second floor. Beside it, to the left, was a small platform. To its left was a small storage area where coal was stored, followed by a bathroom and an Indian-style toilet. Next to it, the courtyard had a door opening into the side lane. Underneath the staircase was a storage area and to its right, behind the office, was another tiny room. This was the servant's room. The staircase made a right-angle turn and ended at a doorway with iron bars.

Immediately to the left was the entrance to a kitchen and pantry. A gallery went past a room above the living room and made a right turn at the entrance to the corner room. It went past a toilet and bathroom to the steps going to the third floor. Two rooms fronted the main lane with an iron mesh enclosed balcony with two windows. The first room was a utility room, and the second, a bit larger, was my mother's room, with several in-the-wall closets, a high cornice running on all the walls, and a tiny attic storage area. At the end of the gallery, steep steps lead to the third floor. There, an open-air toilet was on the right, and on the left, a grille of iron bars (tattar) formed the cover for the open space down to the first-floor courtyard. The rest of the roof was enclosed by a four-foot-high parapet. There were two steps leading up to a room above the kitchen area with windows at the front and to the open roof. This was a utility room, used as a guest bedroom, to move in when it rained when we slept on the roof, and for storage. Open sandstone steps jutting out of the back wall led to the flat roof above, which had a low parapet.

There was a spectacular view of the city from here. The top of the back wall was covered with jagged glass shards embedded in plaster. This was to prevent intrusion from the roof of the house in the back but primarily to prevent feral rhesus monkeys, who roamed in small troops on roofs all over town. The house was built in an area of about 60 x 40 feet! All houses were made of solid brick or stone with cement and plaster. Wood was used only for doors and windows.

Across the front door was the municipal public water station at the end of a lane. This was a shallow stone quadrangle with four faucets coming out of a squat hydrant, one in each direction. It was always a hub of activity from dawn till late at night, with mostly women conversing loudly, sometimes arguing and quarreling while filling their metal or clay containers. The lane across from us led to a poor neighborhood where there was no municipal water supply. Across, to the left, was a small open area with a hut and several cows and water buffalo, and a pen. Next to that was a five or six storied small building, with a doctor's office to one side. The lane then curved out of view. Across to the right was a small thatched hut in an open enclosure.

Next was a lane at the end of which lived Maulvi saheb (a Muslim scholar), who taught Arabic, Persian, and Urdu at St. John's college. The main lane curved to the right and had a snack and sweet shop followed by a large pan-cigarette shop. Right after our house, on the corner of the side lane, was a house with a tailor shop at street level. The lane went behind our house and dead-ended into an open area fronting several houses. There were innumerable lanes opening into the main lane till it ended into the main road at each end. The main lane was made of large sandstone blocks, with shallow angular open drains on both sides. Our neighborhood was called Moti Katra.

The lanes were swept, and the drains were cleaned by municipal sweepers early each morning. They also emptied the waste buckets (night soil) from the bathrooms of each house, which had openings into the lanes, and wheeled the night soil away in wooden carts. Street lights were sparsely placed and gave poor illumination. The main lane was always bustling with pedestrians, pushcarts, tongas, bicycles, mules bearing all kinds of freight, stray cows, bulls, and dogs. Add to this the frequent religious, funeral, marriage, and political processions.

My dad was building a house outside the city, so my grandfather (Baba) was staying with us to supervise the construction. Occasionally I would go to the site with him. At the end of the day, he would pay the workers and keep an account. I remember a laborer, Jas Ram, who later became our mason for projects at the house later on. I think the laborers got 2 annas (about 9cents) and a mason 8 annas a day

Every evening, Kanahia, the milkman from across our house, would pass by hawking his homemade ice cream from an all- wooden three-wheeled push cart. Baba would buy me one for a paisa (pice) (1/64th of a rupee). It came out as a cone from a large clay pot surrounded by ice covered with burlap and served in a dona (two large dried leaves sewn together as a cone with twigs). About two weeks later, I came down with a fever, which was not unusual, as all kinds of infectious diseases were common. After a few days, Dr. Gurumukh Ram Tandon came to see me and diagnosed it as Typhoid. He was a short, good-looking, plump man with a ruddy complexion, and wore a round, brown, felt topi (cap). There were no antibiotics or cures. You either died or recovered. Though most people recovered, there was still a significant mortality rate.

I was given some medicine, and strict orders were given not to feed me any solid food. I was on a fruit juice, diluted milk, and water diet. A cot was placed for me in the front guest room. I was ravenously hungry all the time. One day a parcel came from my Nani (maternal grandmother) with, as usual, homemade snacks. I stole several goodies and placed them under my pillow, and ate them when I was alone. My Nani sent a large parcel of goodies and some clothes for mom and Sidya Bahen every two weeks or so. It took me many weeks to recover, and I became very skinny and remained skinny afterward.

I grew up like other Khatri boys, with long hair braided in a single or double ponytail or knotted on top, which was very puzzling to people not used to our tradition of not cutting a boy's hair till the 'Mundan' ceremony at the age of 5 years. This consisted of shaving it all off in a religious ceremony celebrated with relatives and friends. The other ceremony, less elaborate, was 'Patti-puja.' This was the initiation of education. It was marked by worship involving a wooden writing board and reed pens, and chalk paste. I do not remember how far I progressed with that, but in 1944 I was admitted to Kindergarten at St. Anthony's convent school in the Agra Cantonment area, about four miles away. Every morning the servant would take me to school by bicycle, with me sitting on the front bar, and pick me up midafternoon.

I have some memories of the early days. We were taught and made to speak English by female teachers dressed differently (western dress). They were kind, gentle, and caring, and the class was small. I think I learned fast, though I still remember an embarrassing moment. The teacher was teaching us how to tell time using a play clock. She turned the short hand to three and the long hand to six and asked me to tell the time. I said, "Three and a half." Translating literally from the Hindi equivalent. She corrected me gently, but my classmates giggled, and I was embarrassed. I learned not to speak in English till I was sure and learned fast. I also remember a strange but not unpleasant smell coming from the adjoining Nun's kitchen. I later learned it was from the roasting of meat.

The next year I started going to school by tonga (a horse carriage). Friends of my father, the Mehra family, who also sent their children to that school by their tonga, offered me a ride. This involved a quarter of a mile walk to the main street to the left, where I would wait for the tonga. They were three cousins. The oldest sat up front, and the other two sat in the back. I sat to one side in the back. The youngest, Vijay, was in my class. He was nice. We became good friends. Initially, the servant would walk me to the pick-up spot, but after a few days, I became confident in walking by myself. I became adept at negotiating the traffic and learnt the landmarks.

The school was co-educational (boys and girls). The students in school were Anglo- Indians, children of military personnel from the military base, and a few Europeans. I became friends with a freckle-faced boy, Brian. He delighted in modifying the learning of the alphabet from A for apple, B for box to A for atom and B for bomb, and I would join him. I had no idea what those words meant, but we were delighted to have done something different. The education was strictly British, with nursery rhymes of Humpty

Dumpty, Jack Horner, Miss Muffett, and Hickory Dickory Dock, singing Three Blind mice, Ring around the rosy, learning about Robin Hood, Jack and the beanstalk and Alice in Wonderland. I was learning and speaking English at school and spoke regular Hindi with everyone but the Kannauj dialect with the family.

I also became familiar with the route to and from school. The congested road opens up at the Criminal courts complex, then the small replica of the Taj Mahal at the Habib Bank building after an overpass, followed by the Imperial Hotel, the large sign of Ganeshi Lal & Sons, the Collector's house on the right, the long low boundary wall of the Laurie's Hotel after that, then a right angle turn to the left leading to the school. I mention this not only to tell you about these old landmarks but also about what happened one day.

There was a designated area in front of the school where several tongas, even a buggy, one or two cars, and a few bicycles waited to pick up children after school. One afternoon as I came out to go for my ride, I did not see the tonga, nor did I see my fellow passengers. I looked around and waited. When all the waiting vehicles had left, I looked back at the school building. There was nobody around for me to tell them I had no ride home. I started crying softly, for I was afraid, and started to walk slowly to the gate, a few hundred feet away. I looked around. There was no tonga waiting for me. I strapped my bag to my back and started walking towards home. I stayed well away from the tarred road, walking on the dirt shoulder. Carefully, I crossed over to Laurie's hotel boundary wall. It started to drizzle. I kept walking, occasionally looking up at the passing tongas in the hope that one of them might be my ride.

After a while, I just walked and tried not to look. I followed my familiar landmarks and reached home soaking wet. At home, my mother was waiting, extremely worried. They had not yet panicked about my return as sometimes we were late coming back for various reasons, but never this late. I explained to my mother what had happened, and she was not happy. It was the first time that I saw her complain to my father about anything. She even suggested that I start being transported by the servant again. But nothing happened. The next day I asked Vijay's brother about leaving me behind. He said that they waited for me, and when I did not show up after a while, they left. Vijay was absent that day. I did not want to argue over the matter and dropped the subject.

My father was an anglicized Indian when out of the house. His routine was, getting dressed in pants, tie and jacket, or a suit, after a very early lunch, just before 10 a.m.

He also wore a stiff detachable collar and cuffed shirts. He came down from upstairs, and the servant held his bicycle, freshly cleaned, wiped his shoes, and he went off to the college (his place of work). After college, he went to the staff club, where he played tennis and came back around 5 p.m. The servant waited for him and took care of the bicycle. He would then change and have a snack. Invariably it would include people dropping in. We had visitors all evening long. Students, friends, and some seeking favors. Sometimes he would ask for tea and snacks for some visitors, and mom would send them down with the servant. He would come up to have dinner around 8 or 9 p.m. He was very social outside but stern at home. Everyone at home was deferential to him and even afraid of him, as he had a reputation for having a short temper which flared fast and ebbed fast too. He was the neighborhood air-raid warden for World War II. We had many flat canvas fire hoses and canvas belts, and water buckets stored in our house.

The Udaya Shankar (older brother of Ravi Shankar, the famous sitar player) dance ballet came to town, and my father had nearly all of them come over for lunch one day. There must have been at least twenty of them. We got complimentary tickets for their show. It had some spectacular dance-dramas which I did not understand.

My mother was a short but good-looking, soft-spoken, quiet, hardworking, and talented woman. She had a basic education and knew the English alphabet and numerals but could not speak or write English. She spoke the Shahjahanpuri dialect of Hindi, very similar to the one of Kannauj. She woke up before everyone else in the morning and took her bath, and did a brief puja (worship) in the corner of her room, where she had the pictures of the Hindu deities and the tiny utensils needed for the puja. By that time, the servant was up too, and the two got busy making breakfast and the preparations for lunch. Breakfast was hot milk in the winter and lassi (a yogurt drink) in the summer, with homemade snacks. We did not drink tea. We ate individually. There was no sitting together. After my father had his breakfast, he went down to his office to work, as Sidya Bahen and I got ready for school. We carried our lunch in a small metal container and our books. My dad would finish his work, get ready and have the freshly prepared early lunch and leave for college. My mom then did her formal puja, which consisted of reading the Ramayana by Tulsidas very softly near the icons. Before I started going to school, I would listen, sitting next to her. I had memorized a respectable number of verses by the time I was ready for school. She would then start some projects like sewing, knitting, pickling, making paapar (lentil wafer), sifting grain, or pounding or grinding spices. She had lunch and read the Kalyan, a religious magazine, and snoozed a little. It was then time to start preparing for dinner, which was around 8 p.m. She was the last person to eat at night after serving the servant. This is what every middle-class woman did. She did not have much social interaction except with the wife of the neighbor to our left.

She had a moderate-sized wooden box with labeled compartments in it, containing paper and coin currency, in her cupboard. It was her version of the budget allotment for household expenses. It had a lock that opened by lining up the code word. She seemed to be secretive about it and unlocked it with no one around. I was curious. One day, as she was manipulating the lock to line up the code word, I sneaked up behind her shoulder and read it-U-N-U-S-E-D. I gleefully ran around upstairs and downstairs, repeating "U-N-U-S-E-D," much to the puzzlement of everyone and to my mother's face expressing annoyance and amusement at the same time.

Some of my father's large social circle became part of the family. They were all addressed as chacha or mama (father's younger brother or mother's younger brother) and would come upstairs freely to interact with us. Nemi chacha and Padam chacha are the two I remember most. Nemi chacha was good-looking and affable from a local banya (traders) family. Padam chacha was also good-looking but earnest, from a banya (trading) family, and was attending St. John's college. Both lived close by. Padam chacha would come daily after college and stay till late.

The house my father had built outside the old city was ready, but we could not move in as it got billeted, for the war was going on, and housing for non-Indians, outside the city, was in short supply. I think the house was completed in 1944 and got rented to a Czechoslovakian in charge of a potato products factory.

The news came (by postcard) that chachi's (my paternal uncle's wife) brother Kanhai mama got arrested and was sentenced to six months in jail. He was a freedom fighter in the ongoing struggle in the country for Independence from British colonial rule. I remember the episode, for, after hearing the news, I was coming down from the roof beating my chest and exclaiming, "Inqalab Zindabad" (long live the revolution), in imitation of the freedom fighters, slipped, and came tumbling down the steep, stone steps. I was stunned and cried. I had multiple bruises on my head and face, which took some time to heal.

Giving sweets to friends during major religious festivals was an old Indian tradition. During the Muslim festival of

Eid, we would get some from Maulvi saheb, our neighbor mentioned earlier. One of the treats was Sayvaeen. These were thin noodles cooked in sweetened milk. I loved it. This was my first introduction to Muslim dessert. We also sent over sweets to his family during Diwali. During Muharram, a long procession carrying Tajias (replicas of buildings) was carried out by the Shia sect of Muslims, with some beating their chests, some self-flagellating and wailing and mourning for the prophets Hassan and Hussain.

Suddenly, one day, there was great celebration and joy, both outside and inside the house. I asked Sidya Bahen why everyone was celebrating. News of victory over Japan had arrived. People were talking of the war coming to an end. In the evening, we went up to the top roof and heard and saw the fireworks in the distance-celebrations going on at the military bases. It was spectacular. These were the first fireworks I had ever seen.

A couple, the Joshis, came to stay with us for a few months. I think Mrs. Joshi was finishing up her Master's degree. She was the daughter of Dr. Pant from Bareilly. Our families became close. His eldest son, Girish, whom we called mama (mother's brother), also came and stayed with us for a few days and then got accepted at Agra Medical College. He would visit us often on weekends. Dr. Pant sent us a radio. Radio was a rare novelty. It was placed in mom's room in a corner. It was about a 2x1 foot brown box with round knobs and a dial in the front. R C A was imprinted above the dial. Neighbors came to look at it. The servant was puzzled as to how voices and music came out of a box. My father would listen to the news in the morning. My sister and I listened to a children's program on Sunday mornings. It could be switched to medium or short wave and dialed to receive broadcasting stations. Mostly we left it tuned to New Delhi, for the rest of the stations were full of static. The reception was better in the evening than in the daytime.

I accompanied Padam chacha to a few local wedding dinner parties when my dad could not go. The process of feasting was called 'Jeemna.' These parties were a model of adaptation and efficiency. The inner city houses were small, and the number of invitees was large, yet a perfectly working, seamless way was worked out. People would arrive and would be seated on chairs on the lower floors or in the lane/street. One corner or side of the roof would be the open kitchen, where most of the food was cooked. All along the other three sides, a three-foot wide sheet was laid down for the first group of guests to sit on. Servers brought out 'pattals' (round mats made from large dry leaves knitted together with twigs) and placed one in front of each person. Then came the baked clay 'kulhar' (oval container) and ‘sakoras’ (small bowls) of the same material. Then came a person with a ‘gangasagar’ (a metal container with a narrow spout) and poured a little water from it into the kulhar and the sakoras. The guests swished the water around in them to get any clay dust off and emptied them in the back or front. Then came the dishes in metal containers.’ Bundi-ka-raita’ (a yogurt dish), ‘rassay-ki-sabzi’ (vegetable with gravy), ‘lapatay-ke-aloo’ (potatoes in thick paste), other vegetables, ‘puri’ (fried flat bread), ’kachaouri’ (small stuffed fried bread), ‘sonth’ (a kind of relish) and three, five or seven kinds of ‘mithai’ (desserts), which depended on the financial situation of the host. Once everything was served, people would start eating. Servers would come by frequently to replenish anything you wanted except the mithai. Padam chacha taught me not to gorge on the courses and save my appetite to enjoy the desserts.

When this group was finished eating, they moved out, the containers were picked up, the area was washed lightly, and the next group was seated till everyone was fed. On the way out, pan, ‘supari’ (areca nuts), cardamom, peppermint, and tobacco, were offered. The uneaten food was fed to the stray cows and the unsoiled to the bhangis (refuse removers). Nearly all workers except the cooks were volunteer friends and relatives of the host. Nothing became garbage, and everything was used or biodegradable. This environmentally friendly dinner went the way of the dinosaurs once people started moving out of the inner city and with Westernization.

Ever since I could remember, we had a live-in servant. All came from the Kumaon-Garhwal area at the foothills of the Himalayas for the area was very poor. The servant went home for a week or two every one or two years. He was treated well and taken care of. In my childhood, it was Dharam Singh, and I have vague memories of him. I remember he took me to one of the roadside photographers behind the hospital, and we had our picture taken. When I grew older, I heard my parents talk of Dilip. Apparently, he was the servant before Dharam Singh. My father taught him to read and write, and trained him, so he became adept at almost everything to be done at home. He even did all the monetary transactions at the post office, where his name was in a joint account with my Dad's. In those days, the post office also did savings accounts and monetary transactions, like the banks. After many years he contracted TB and died while my father was away on tour. He was at a temple in South India where only Brahmins were allowed in the sanctum. The priest would ask for your Gotra (lineage name) before letting you in. My father, wanting to go in, gave them a Brahmin one, and was admitted. Father learned of Dilip's death when he returned and was distraught. He took it as a punishment from God for lying at the temple. Dilip's name frequently came up when my parents reminisced, for he seemed to be much loved. TB had a worse effect on people coming from the Foothills, as unlike in the plains, it was not common there, so they had no immunity (herd immunity). People who had Tb were isolated in sanatoria, usually located out of town in open areas, in the belief that fresh air would help with the recovery and also prevent transmission. Treatment was supportive care, as there was no cure for it.

Sometime in late 1945 or early 1946, my father was admitted to the hospital. My uncle came from Kannauj. Everyone was concerned and grim, but the reason was never talked about, then and even later. I suspect that he had a mild nervous breakdown as when he came back from the hospital, he did not look physically changed, but his way of living did. He stopped wearing a tie. Except for college, he started to wear a kurta (Indian shirt) and dhoti (Indian lower garment) made of khadi (homespun) cotton yarn, wear non-leather shoes called go-rakshak (cow savers), and a Gandhi cap. A vigorous Independence movement under the leadership of Mahatma Gandhi had been going on for decades, home-spun clothing and the cap were its uniforms. Hindu-Muslim riots started occurring sporadically as there was a movement to form a breakaway country by some Muslims – Pakistan.

The Move

In 1946 we moved to our newly built house as the tenant vacated it. My uncle came from Kannauj to help. The house was designed by Sharma saheb, my father's close friend and professor of English at St. John's College. He was a short, dark man who was totally anglicized. He had a modern house, near ours, with a lawn, a lily pond, a gazebo and a Ford car. His wife was affable and social. They grew flowers and won prizes at the local flower show at Agra Club. They had no children. Our house was a departure from the usual Indian design of a central courtyard surrounded by corridors into which rooms opened. I will describe the layout in detail.

A small gate and a short path led to three long steps wrapped around a curved verandah which had twin mosaic pillars. The verandah curved back on the left to the door of a small room. A drawing room to the right, a room in the front with a window and a door to a gallery in between, which ran through the depth of the house. In the right front corner was a room with two adjacent windows. The back of this room opened by a door onto a verandah. The verandah was open on the right, leading down three stone steps along its length into the courtyard. The kitchen was at the other end of the verandah. On its left, there was a window and a door leading to the family room, which was directly behind the drawing room and its exact duplicate, with a fireplace and a shared chimney. At the end of the verandah on the left was a door to a passageway which joined the main gallery of the house.

The front room had two windows opening into the left side of the verandah and a door in the back to an open space in the middle of the gallery. Into it flowed a wide staircase from the left with a solid smooth balustrade on its right. Straight ahead from the foot of the staircase was a door leading to a room with a window on the back wall and one on its left wall. There was a door on this wall, and both the window and the door opened into a verandah. The verandah was open in the back and on the left, where a small door connected it to a tiny room with a window. Two adjacent doors connected it to the front verandah and to the house interior beside the balustrade. Underneath the balustrade, near this door, was a small alcove with a door.

The gallery was connected to the back passageway by a door. The floor here consisted of a wooden door which covered the steps leading to the basement, which was under the back verandah and had two ventilators opening under its steps. The passageway was connected to the family room by a door on its right and by one on its left to the storage room or pantry, which was connected to the kitchen. The back end of the gallery had a bathroom and a toilet with separate doors and a partial wall separating them. The end of the gallery had a door which opened onto a three-foot-high platform around the back of the house. Three steps from it lead to the alley which separated it from the house in the back.

The staircase led up to a wide landing with a tall roof and its walls consisting of three large full-length windows, each consisting of small glass panes, right up to the fifteen feet ceiling, lighting up and warming that side of the interior of the house, since it was the south side. It gave a magnificent effect both from the inside and the outside. The staircase made a smooth hairpin turn and ended up on a smaller landing which had a door opening to each of the three sides onto a flat roof. All along the roof was a well-designed wide parapet with a continuous see-through ornate design. In the middle was a covered raised rectangle, about four feet high, the fireplace chimney.

The entire flooring was mosaic, as were the front pillars, with different colors inlay designs, in each room. The courtyard was fenced in by a brick wall about five feet high. On the left side of the house, there was a four-foot space and another four-foot wall separating it from the house next door. There was a small lawn in the front of the house with a water faucet near the right front. A five-foot high brick wall and bougainvillea vines separated the house from the road. A small guava tree stood across from the drawing room.

The house was much more spacious and aesthetically pleasing than the one we moved from. There was hardly any traffic except for the few tongas and bicycles in the daytime, and practically none in the evening, when the civil courts, about half a mile up the road, closed for the day. This was in stark contrast to the noisy hustle-bustle of the inner city, which I was used to. The only place which had any shops was near the civil courts. It consisted of a chakki (small flour mill), a pan-cigarette seller, and a shop selling milk, yogurt, and some dairy-based sweets. Towards the other end of the road, about a couple of hundred yards away from the house, was another pan-beetle-cigarette shop which also sold bottles of soda and, in summer, ice. So it was quite a change, if not a jolt- our moving from the city.

A few weeks after our move to the new house, news of Hindu-Muslim riots and looting in the city and in many other parts of the country was in the papers and on the radio. It was calm and quiet in our area. One day my father made us assemble around the radio and asked us to be quiet and listen. Soon Jawaharlal Lal Nehru, respectfully called Pandit ji, came on the air and gave a speech in English. My father looked somber and visibly moved. I didn't quite follow, but later understood that it was a historic day, of partition of the country and Independence from Britain. It was August 15 1947. My father made us place a few lit earthenware lamps (diyas) on the parapet of the roof. I think there were some fireworks displays downtown, but otherwise, nothing changed, and we did not feel any different.

We inherited a Siamese cat left by the previous resident. It was all black and surprisingly accepted by my mother, who was very particular about her kitchen and pooja area not being defiled by any animal. It roamed the neighborhood, and soon we had several kittens who became feral. The cats kept the mice, which infested every house, in check.

St. Peter's College

My father got me admitted to St. Peter's College, which was about a mile away to our east. This was also a Catholic school with the same schedule as St. Anthony's, so the transfer was practically seamless. I joined the second standard, as the academic session for 1947 had just started. After a few days of being escorted by the servant, I learnt the way to school and walked there on my own.

From the main road, at the pan shop mentioned earlier, the road branched east and straight ahead with a low brick wall encircling the hills on the left and a large space followed by a very high (about16') wall of the Central jail on the right. This wall continued straight ahead. On the left, there were several houses with small gardens in front. After a gentle up-slope, the road turned slightly right. To the left, there was an old neighborhood called Wazirpura, straight ahead was the entrance gate to a park called Hewitt Park. To its right, between the road and the jail wall, was a large fenced-in water tank, which curved with the road for a few hundred feet. There was a high wall after the park gate that stretched for quite a distance, except for a large gate about a hundred yards further down. On the right, the distance between the road and the jail wall widened; otherwise, they ran parallel to each other for another two hundred yards or so to the large gate of St. Peter's church on the left. There the jail wall made a turn away to the west.

The church building, inset from the gate, was imposing, with a very tall spire. It had two roads encircling it. I took the one on the right. It went past several residential and office buildings on the right to the school building, several hundred yards up. This was a long rectangular, impressive, two-storied building with a large St. Peter's crest and seal, and 'St. Peters College 1846' circumscribing it at the center of the top of the building. There was a small porch in the middle at the front. The road on the left front of the church ran parallel to the one on the right and ended up in front of the school. To me, coming from a modest convent school building, it was awesome.

A few stone steps led to a verandah which went around the entire building. The porch was in front of the Principal's office, and the classrooms of the first, second, and third standards were to the left, each with a central open doorway. At the end of the verandah was a wide staircase curving up to the second floor. The verandah then continued to the back, with a large room on the left, followed by the science section. It then widened considerably as it went past the combined seventh and eighth, the fifth, fourth, sixth and the combined ninth and tenth standard classrooms, followed by a small room.

The dining hall opened into it and to the left was another staircase leading up to the dormitory. Across from the small room were four or five faucets over a curved trough. The back of the verandah opened to another wide area with some benches and then a large playing field. The verandah made a right-angle turn and continued to the front as a corridor, past the back end of a large hall with solid wooden desks and benches- the study hall. This had a stage at the other end. It then joined the front verandah, which went past the study hall to the Principal's office. Each side of the front of the school had an oblong garden surrounded by a low hedge and a fountain at its center.

In front, between the two approach roads, was a long wide depression which had two deteriorating tennis courts. On the other side of the main approach road was another depression and a building which had a kindergarten and a few living quarters. On the right side of the main building was a short covered passageway to a small building which was the clerk's office. Behind this was a path leading to a set of quarters for some teachers. On the left front of the building, next to the other approach road, was the swimming pool and a covered well supplying water for the pool. Adjoining the left side of the school building was a printing press followed by a large playing field. At the west end of the field was another fair-sized building called the Hospital. To its right, in a small depression, was a cottage. At the end of the field on the left was a building where a few teachers lived. The field behind the main building, on its right, had a few steps, leading to a depression which had about a dozen lavatories with open fronts and tin doors covering the lower third.

I joined the second standard, which had about twelve students. Our teacher was a woman whose name I cannot recall. She was big by Indian standards, probably an Anglo-

Indian. Some students referred to her as 'Bumblebee'- out of earshot, of course. We had wooden desks with a slanting top and a long shallow depression in the front and an ink well on the right, and armless wooden chairs. There was a teacher's chair and desk in the front and a large blackboard behind that. On my first day, I was taken to the headmaster's office, who took me to a large deep cupboard at the front of the study hall and gave me my textbooks and stationery. All textbooks and stationery were supplied by the school.

St. Peter's College was a Catholic school founded in 1846 and was also called St. Peter's College and Orphanage, as it housed many orphans. It might have had some postsecondary education at some time. Hence the name 'college'- is my guess. There was a separate sister institution, surrounded by a high wall to the left of the church building- St. Patrick's, a boarding school for girls, and a nunnery. St. Peter's church also had many priests and brothers, but they were not involved in teaching. It was mainly a boarding school. The dormitory was on the second floor of the building. I never got to see it, as day scholars were not allowed there. The school was primarily for the education of British residents and native Christians and was entirely English speaking. The natives were mostly Anglo-Indians and Indian Christians. The term Anglo-Indian was applied to the descendants of actual Anglo-Indians. I saw only two brothers who were actual Anglo-Indians during my entire stay. The Anglo-Indians remained a separate group. They were not fully accepted by the British, did not mingle with Indians and considered themselves a cut above. They were all Christians and followed British traditions in food, music, language, and demeanor and did not assimilate into Indian society. They were favored with jobs in the railway, police, telegraph, telephone, and nursing.

Since the medium for all government and other important matters was English, people who wanted their children to get a leg up sent their children, mostly boys, to such schools. These private schools, run mostly by various Christian denominations, tried to emulate the British 'public schools.' They had their own board of education, and some, like mine, were affiliated with Universities in Britain, which set the curriculum and examinations and awarded a 'senior overseas school certificate' upon graduation. Unlike the local school year, which ran from July to May, ours ran from January to November. Our school was affiliated with Cambridge University, and the graduation exam came from there, and the answer books were sent there. Instead of 'class,' we used the term 'standard.' There was an exam in the eighth standard, which was called the 'Junior School Certificate exam,' also called 'Junior Cambridge' in short. Similarly the senior was called 'Senior Cambridge.' This was equivalent to the first year of the local undergraduate system. A bit confusing? It gets even more interesting. In early standards, we exclusively studied British History and the British currency system in Arithmetic. French and Urdu were dropped when I joined, and there was no Hindi yet.

It took me a few days to get accustomed to the school. School started at 8 a.m. with a short interval (break) at about 10 a.m., then a longer break for lunch around 12 p.m. and ended at 3.30 p.m. Unlike local schools, which had a full day, we had half a day of school on Saturdays. After a few days of being dropped off by the servant by bicycle, I started to walk to school. I walked along the side of the road (there was no sidewalk). There was hardly any traffic except for a few bicycles and an occasional tonga. It took me about twenty minutes each way. There was a school bus, but it was for students who lived further away.

I carried my books in a canvas bag slung from my shoulder. It also had my lunch box. The boarding students, or borders as they were called, ate in the dining room, and we, the day scholars, on the benches behind the school. There was a bell with a rope hanging from the wall between the fourth and sixth standard, and a student from the tenth standard, designated for the purpose, rang the bell at the end of each period and for the breaks. The walk to and from school was very interesting. I made friends with a few students, and we would walk back chatting till the church gate and would part company, as there was no one going in my direction. I walked along the high church and St. Patrick's wall, passed a small grave, then crossed over to the water tank, under a few trees there, crossed over to the other side and then followed the road till it veered right and then the short cut through a small depression, jumped across a small drain and crossed the road near my house. There was always something to see or do, like kicking a can or stone till I lost it, watching a kite soar in the sky or some other distraction on the road. I was never bored. That short walk helped greatly in expanding and enjoying my imagination.

I made many new friends in my class and with others, and I enjoyed going to school. Absence from school necessitated a letter from a parent with the reason for the absence, to the headmaster, before rejoining the class. We had corporal punishment, but I never saw it in class. The one I saw was caning. It was done by the headmaster, in the corridor, just outside his office. More on that later.

One day at the beginning of class, the teacher took me out of the class and led me to the headmaster's office. They talked briefly. He came out and looked at me, went back to his office, came back out, handed me a note, and asked me to go home and give it to my father. I was puzzled but did as he asked. At home, my father, who had still not gone to work, looked at the note, then at me, smiled a little, wrote a note and told me to go back to school and give it to my headmaster. I was still puzzled, but in those days, you did not question but did what the elders told you to do. So back I walked to school and to the headmaster's office and gave him the note. He looked at it, then at me, smiled and gave me a note and told me to go back to the class and give it to my teacher. The teacher read the note, smiled, looked at me, asked me to take my seat and resumed teaching.

Later, when I came home, I told my sister about what had happened and asked if she knew what was going on. By now, everyone in the house knew. She told me that I had mosquito bites all over my face and ears, which the teacher at school thought was measles. She then explained to me what measles was. This time I smiled and went to see in the mirror my red-dotted face! I have always been a magnet for mosquitos, and even if there are others within easy-biting distance, a mosquito will always make a beeline (mosquito-line?) for me!

I started to make more friends. Arnold MacDonald, Gullo, Rajendra, and Prahalad are the ones I remember. They were all-day scholars. The white colored small school bus transported some students living far from school. I do not know what the eligibility criteria were. I enjoyed school. The teacher was nice, and everyone was friendly. I did not know about the boarding system or many borders as yet.

We covered our textbooks and notebooks using old newspapers. This was a practical and prudent thing, for there was dust, grease (from hair oil and food) and wear and tear from usage. These were all in black ink, and would smudge a little. On the cover, we wrote our names in ink. Sometimes we wrote our names on the inside of the textbooks. Some wrote a brief warning to would-be stealers, e. g. 'My book is one thing, my boot another. Steal not the first for fear of the other.' Each desk had an ink well built in the right front top. To the middle of the same area was an oblong depression to keep our 'holders', pencils and rubber erasers. The holder was about a six-inch long wooden pen which tapered at the top. Its lower end had a groove. Into this fitted a thin, slightly curved metal piece with a bifurcated tip called the nib. The nibs came in various shapes and lengths, depending on what was required to be transcribed. This was dipped into the inkwell to pick up the ink to write. So one had to learn how much of it had to be dipped and for how long to avoid splattering ink on the desk or on paper. Since the ink did not dry immediately after writing, blotting papers were used. These were rectangular, coarse, white sheets of paper, to be gently dabbed over the written area, to blot the excess ink and avoid smudges. Most students had ink smudges on their thumb and first two fingers and occasionally on their faces, no matter how careful they were. The pencils did not have erasers at the top. We had separate rubber erasers of various shapes and sizes. The notebooks (exercise books) came lined and unlined. Writing was a subject like English or Arithmetic. The 'Writing' exercise books had two parallel faint gray-blue lines, above which, at a little more distance, was a faint pinkish-red line. The capital and long letters were to extend up to the top line, and the lowercase letters were written between the other two lines. All writing was with a slightly forward incline. Penmanship was taught up to the fourth standard and was important even up to the higher standards and considered a factor when exams were marked. At home, we used slate boards. These were rectangles of slate framed in wood and used a special slate pencil to write. It was easily erasable by the side of the palm or a slightly wet cloth. It came in handy at practicing whatever you wanted to write or practice.

From my classmate Rajendra, I learnt that there was a shortcut to my walk to school. He came from Wazirpura, the neighborhood just outside the Hewett Park gate and across from the water tank I passed every day. He showed me the way. We crossed the field on the left of the school, into the descent near the clerk's cottage, and then through a small opening in a fence, into the park. A few yards led to the road, slightly uphill, to the park gate. This saved at least ten minutes from my commute each way. An added bonus was someone to walk with for a part of the walk back from school.

'The park surrounded the school-church complex, except for a small area to the southeast and was separated from it by a thick, dense wide area of babul (acacia) bushes and trees, forming a nearly impenetrable barrier. This area was out of bounds to us though some senior boarders (boarding students) did gather there during lunch break and after school. These were called 'gangs'. I remember hearing of one called 'Caleb's gang' but never learnt any details, for I had few borders as friends, and they were not part of these. Another activity was of trying to shoot down birds in the babul thickets using slingshots called 'catties'. These were hand-made from babul branches, scavenged elastic rubber and leather strips and twine.

Across from the left side of the school was an open-air swimming pool. This was about thirty feet long and fifteen feet wide, and five feet deep, made of large slabs of sandstone blocks. To its left was a small building which housed the well and pumps supplying water for the pool. The pool was used during late spring and summer. Near it, toward the field, was a room labeled 'The Tuck Shop'. It sold peanut brittle and some other dry snacks during certain hours. It used school currency, which was metal coins with denominations in annas stamped on them. The boarders got the pocket money given by their parents in school currency every week. This was done apparently to prevent students from sneaking out to buy things from outside. Going out of bounds was prohibited for borders. I think some students were given permission to go out occasionally.

My knowledge of the boarders routine was what I learned from them. There was a separate dormitory hall for older boys, and there was a 'lights out' and sleeping time supervised by a priest or brother. School started after breakfast. Lunch was at noon, and tea was after school. Dinner was after washing up after sports in the evening, followed by a supervised study hall for two hours to study and do homework. All meals were the Western style. I suspect the meals were either not sufficient, or the growing boys required more, for boarders often asked their day scholar friends to share their lunch or bring something from home. Once a week, I think on Saturdays, they got a dose of castor oil. Sick boys were sent to the 'Hospital' building to be seen by Mr. Pasquale, who was in charge. Sicker ones were admitted, as there were, I think, eight or ten beds in the building. Once or twice a week, or as necessary, a doctor came in to see the sick. Mr. Pasquale also dispensed medicines.

Neighborhood

The neighborhood consisted of the large gate of the Bharatpur State Agent's residence across from us. To our left lived a widow with her two teenage daughters. Behind us, separated by a lane, was a two-storied house with a garden. The garden had guava and tangerine trees and was separated from the lane by a seven-foot-high wall. The house had a small open courtyard and an outside staircase leading to the top floor. The western or back end was occupied by the owner- Pathak ji. He was the priest to the Maharaja of Avagarh, was a widower, and lived with his widowed sister (Bua ji) and son. The rest of the house was rented to two brothers with a large family of children of all ages- the Choubey Ji's. In the house next to them lived Govindji, also with a large family and children of all ages. He was the general manager of the Swadeshi Bima Company. The lane opened into the main street of the development (colony), which led a few hundred feet further west to the Company building. There were several houses to the sides and behind this. This was the Swadeshi Bima Nagar Colony. To the south, about a hundred yards from our house, the road surrounding the southwest of the Colony joined the main road. At this corner, there was the Masonic lodge building and a small shop that sold pans, soda water, and, in the summer, ice. Beyond that, across the road, was a low brick wall topped by a barbed wire fence. Between this and the Jail wall was a very large and deep water tank. Across from which on the right was a large hill with a thatched- roof house at its top. To the right of our house was a large open area centered by a large Peepal (fig family) tree and a building which was a girls day school- Normal School.

I soon made friends with a few boys in the neighborhood. After school, we would gather and play in the open area in front of the Bima Company building. Since there was hardly any traffic after 5 p.m., we sometimes played by the side of the main road. Govindji had six sons ranging in age from one to sixteen years. The boys closer to my age had a small bicycle. I learned how to ride on that, and we would go up and down the main road trying to ride without hands and do wheelies, at times crashing and skinning our palms or knees. We also played cricket, soccer, and field hockey. Nearly always, there was a guard at the Bharatpur compound gate across the street. When he was not there, we would knock down bunches of tamarinds from the large trees there. In the rainy season, we would float paper boats we made, on the fast-flowing knee-deep water on the road, till they got wet and sank, or just splashed each other. Or we would chase a wire ring or an old tire-less bicycle wheel propelled with a short stick. None of our games required any elaborate equipment except cricket. Most games involved ages 8 to 18 yrs. playing together. Occasionally we played in the alley behind our house.

Pathakji's fenced-in garden was fair game when the fruit ripened. Some of us would sneak over the fence to pick them.

His widowed sister, Buaji, kept an eye for vandals like us and would yell and chase us away when she heard us in the garden. Forbidden fruit never tasted so sweet- as those guavas! We were not the only interlopers. Black-faced langur monkeys from the nearby Awagarh house would also invade at times, whom Buaji would chase away by making loud noises and brandishing a pole.

Winter was a lot colder at our new home due to the open space as compared to the congested inner city we moved from. Besides, there was no insulation in the brick walls, and all doors had some space between them and the floor for easy clearance, which caused a continuous draft. We did not use the fireplace. On very cold nights, a brazier would be placed in the family room, and we would sit around it at night. This seldom included my father, for he was either in the verandah or in his office with visitors, of which there were many throughout the evening. It was the custom, Victorian or Indian, that men of the older generation did not mingle with the younger most of the time, at least in my family. There was practically no traffic in front of the house. On windy nights we could hear the wind rushing through the trees and the howling of the jackals from the hills across the house, making it feel eerie, especially if we were in the verandah.

Summer time was bad. The temperature would climb as high as 110F in the afternoon. We had a ceiling fan in the family room and one in the drawing room. My father had a 14” black Mitsubishi table fan in his office. Another, a Merelli, was moved around the house where needed. Hand fans of all shapes and sizes, made from woven plant fiber, were used too. At night we slept on the roof, and any male guests would sleep on the lawn. On most nights, it cooled off, but some nights a hot wind would blow from the nearby desert of Rajasthan, making sleep difficult, if not impossible. We slept on cots made of bamboo pole frames (charpai or khatiya) strung with a woven fiber called ‘moonj.’ In the morning, the bedding would be rolled up and piled up in the shade, and the charpais on their sides in one corner of the roof. On top of the platform over the chimney was placed a ‘surahi’ with a metal tumbler covering its top to prevent insects from going in. A surahi was a baked clay container with a small base and a large round body topped by a short narrow neck. It was surprising how cool the water became in it. This was for drinking water at night. Next to it, my mom would put containers of parathas and other food leftover from dinner, covered with a sieve, as we occasionally had that for breakfast, or it was given to the servant. That was our open-air fridge! Occasionally it would start to rain, and we would roll up our beddings and head downstairs and try to sleep on the verandahs, for the rooms were too hot.

An ex-student of my father had an ice factory. He had a relative living close to us and used to send us a slab of ice covered in sawdust and wrapped in a burlap bag by a horse wagon. Ice could be bought in the summer from the panwala shops in small amounts, as it was expensive. We had a small ice cream-making machine. It was a wooden bucket that had an aluminum container in the center and space for packing ice around it, and a handle on one side. We filled the container with thickened, sweetened milk, took turns to turn the handle and in about forty-five minutes had delicious 'ice cream.' Another way of making it was to place milk in empty fifty- cigarette tin cans, seal the lids with dough and pack them randomly in a ghara (round baked clay container) filled with ice chips. We would cover the ghara with burlap and gently rock it in a circular motion, taking turns, as we sat around it and chatted. Again, in about forty-five minutes, we would enjoy the frozen milk we called ice cream.

At night we would tell or listen to stories, especially when my grandmother and cousins were visiting, either by my sister or grandma. Or we would lie on our beds and look at the stars and try to identify the pole star (Dhruv Tara) or the 'seven sisters.' Sometimes, waking up at night, we would hear the loud gong of the nearby Central Jail, which was rung loudly every hour. The number of gongs denoted the hour. At times, on dark nights, the branches of the huge Peepal tree at the Normal School would sway and make scary noises with the wind. In the daytime, the heat started around nine in the morning, reaching its peak around two in the afternoon. No one left the house or shade unless it was absolutely essential, and then with an umbrella. We would take refuge in the basement and take an afternoon nap or play cards or board games and not come up till about 4 p.m. for 'sherbet' (sugar water flavored with rose-water essence) and ice, if it was available.

The rainy season started when the monsoon arrived. This could be anywhere from the end of June or early July and last through September. It was the season welcomed with mixed feelings. When there was a slow breeze with a fine drizzle, it felt heavenly, for it washed away the heat and felt pleasant and invigorating. A few peacocks at the Normal School would come out and call and strut with their feathers spread in beautiful and colorful fans. The cuckoos (koyal) would sing from the trees in joy, welcoming the change of weather. During downpours, we would enjoy seeing it come down in sheets and spray us as we sat on the front verandah, enjoying seeing the sight of people scurrying in the rain, some drenched and others holding on tight to umbrellas wanting to take off with the gusts. As mentioned earlier, we would go on the road and race our paper boats or just frolic in the ankle or knee-deep water with mud between our toes. Mother would make small fritters (Pakoras) of potato and other vegetables in chickpea flour, and we would gobble them down faster than she could fry them. On other days it seemed awful. It would be hot and humid with no breeze and no rain. There were bugs of all sorts, mosquitos, and persistently annoying house-flies flying around- seemingly everywhere. The sweat would drench the clothes and would not dry. The towels remained wet and would start smelling awful. At night there were bugs flying around the naked light bulbs and sometimes dived into the food. Flies multiplied. It would become hard to sleep at night, for the sheets clung to the body. I lost my appetite. I hated those days- and there were lots of them during the season. Gradually the misery abated as everything gradually turned from summer arid to vibrant green.

When it rained heavier than usual, there would be floods. Agra was on the banks of one of the larger rivers of India-the Jumna (Yamuna). The communities right on its banks would flood. When it was unusually large, some of us would go down to see the spectacle. Older boys would take us, the younger ones, riding on the carriers on the back or the bar in front, on their bicycles. It was only a couple of miles away. We would see the boats on the river Jumna's now muddied water and the road on the bank, covered by it, and people going about their business with the lower garments rolled up.

This was also the time for fairs and picnics.

It seemed nearly every week that there was a fair (mela). The fairs were held near, at, or around some holy shrine. We had one at the crossroads near our house and one around a chatri (a round building with a covered verandah open to the outside) behind our development. There were lots of vendors selling balloons, noisemakers, rattles, whirly-gigs, and toys made of baked clay, paper, and reeds. Street food called 'Chat' was plentiful, along with all kinds of sweets. Toy vendors had their wares spread out on cloth sheets over the dirt sidewalk or the grass. Food was sold off wooden carts or large wicker baskets sitting on elongated dumb-bell-shaped stands made of reeds. At bigger fairs, there were Ferris wheels and merry-go-rounds. These were all wood structures and were hand propelled by an operator. Not far from us, about four miles to the north, was the famous Kailash mela around a Shiva temple on the banks of the Jumna. Also, Sheetla Devi, around the temple of a minor but popular deity. I remember going only once to these. They had several thousand participants, mostly women and children from the surrounding villages, with the procession of the deity at the start.

Picnics were mostly an all-male affair, held at gardens or orchards maintained and owned by a wealthy person or community. These were private gatherings of family and friends who would go on their bicycle or tonga (horse carriage), at times called 'dal-bati' (lentils and thick round baked bread), and named after the main course. The venue always had a small building and a well. Everyone had assigned tasks based on their expertise. It started in the morning with the assembling of the cookware and ingredients of the food. Bati makers would prepare the dough. An area on the ground would be marked off, and a thick layer of coke or firewood was ignited and spread out. The dough was shaped into fist size balls, flattened a little, and buried in a shallow covering of the embers of the fire. Lentils (Urad dal) were slow-cooked on an open oven made by propping up a few bricks. Potatoes in a thick spicy gravy (lapaytay kay aloo) would cook on a separate oven. In another area, on a flat, serrated stone slab, were placed the ingredients for a drink called 'Thandai,' literally - 'coolant.'

These were various spices- cardamom, black peppercorns, saffron, ginger, and almonds. They were crushed and powdered by a round or rectangular stone on the stone slab (sil-batta). When the ingredients were super-fine, water was added to make it into a paste. This paste was then slowly dissolved in a thick piece of cloth, partially submerged, in a bucket that had cool water from the well. Sometimes a separate paste was made with a little bhang (cannabis) for its aficionados and dissolved in a different container. You could tell the difference by looking at the color of the thandai. Regular was brownish and the other greenish. Picnickers bathed at the well after the exertion of cooking and then sat down on sheets on the ground to enjoy the feast served on platters made of large dried leaves stitched together with twigs, called 'pattals.' The batis (bread) were retrieved from the embers, dusted off, cracked open a little at the top, and ghee (clarified butter) was poured into the crack. The dal was doused with ghee. As I remember, the inside of the bati was never cooked through. But I guess that is how it was supposed to be, for I never heard anyone complain or discard any portion. The thandai felt cool and spicy, even though there was no ice in it. Well, water, perhaps? But the whole thing was relaxing and enjoyable, especially for the residents of the congested, crowded, hot, and noisy city.

On certain Hindu festivals, my mother would walk to the Jumna, about two miles away, in the company of neighbor women and pray and take a dip there. There were separate ghats (a place to bathe) for men and women. Women bathed and submerged fully clothed and changed into dry clothes at shielded areas. Occasionally I would go with her.

Once, about eight or ten boys in the neighborhood decided to go to another ghat about eight miles away for a bath and swim. We ranged from ten to eighteen years of age. This was a minor shrine with steps and low turrets at the edge of the water. Here the water flowed at a much faster speed than the meandering river in the city. Since everyone except me knew how to swim, one by one, they dove in from one of the turrets after telling me to stay put. I saw them swimming, frolicking, going under, and then coming up. It seemed so simple and easy and inviting. I reasoned that if I jumped on the back of one of them as they swam by, it would be a great ride. As I was contemplating this, mesmerized by the tantalizing current of the river, Prem, one of the neighbors behind our house, came swimming by. As he came below the turret, I jumped to ride on his back. The next thing I remember was choking and coughing violently, lying flat on my back on the ghat. Lucky for me that someone saw me as I came up and submerged a couple of times, dove in, and pulled me out. When I recovered, I got thoroughly rebuked by everyone and given strict orders, not to mention the incident to anyone at home, for my father and others would have given everyone hell. I kept my word and stayed clear of the Jumna for a long time.

Autumn or fall brought relief from the humidity but also a profusion of mosquitoes and flies and a surge in 'viral' fevers and malaria. The villagers used smoke from the burning of dried cow dung discs and dried leaves to drive them away. In cities and towns, people used a metal syringe attached to a small drum (Flit gun) to spray D.D.T. to control these pests. It cooled down noticeably in the morning and evening, and we changed to wearing sweaters and sleeping indoors, starting about Dussehra.

It became cooler around Diwali, and the woolens came out for the winter. Sometimes it would become really cold, and there would be frost on the ground in December and January. People wound scarves around their necks and sometimes even wore gloves, head covers (kantopa), and overcoats. Days were pleasant and sunny in the afternoon, and people sat in the sun for warmth. (Not to tan!). Fields would be ready for harvesting, and mustard fields turned a bright yellow in the countryside for miles; doors would be kept closed, and sometimes coal-fired braziers (angithi) would be used under a cot (charpai) to stay warm. The houses were not insulated, and the space between the floor and the door made them drafty.

The World of My Childhood

The houses on the main road in front of our house (Drummond Road) were called Civil Lines. So our address was 88 'Civil Lines.' During the summer, a horse-drawn municipal water wagon would drive by early morning and afternoon. At its lower back, it had a fenestrated bar that would spray water on the wide unpaved sides of the road in the Civil Lines area to tamp down the dust. This stopped about a year after we moved in. Early in the morning, about 4 a.m., another horse-drawn wagon drove by delivering milk in bottles, small cartons of cream, and packets of butter. This was from the Military dairy-farm doing business with civilians. This was a high-quality, unadulterated, pasteurized product, more expensive than the market fare, and delivered to select customers. The market or civilian milk was 'watered' or otherwise adulterated. Butter came in two forms. Milk-colored and solid, or slightly yellowish salty and softer. Nearly everyone in the neighborhood who did not have a cow or a buffalo had it delivered by milk-men carrying it in a cloth-covered bucket and doling it out with a long-handled ladle. Like the spray wagon, the military dairy delivery also stopped after a while. A civilian dairy, 'Singhal Dairy,' started delivering milk from tanks on the back of bicycles.

For a few years, we had rationing of essentials like sugar, wheat, and gasoline (petrol). Every household had a ration card and could go to the ration shop to get their allotted amount at a controlled price. The same commodities were also available at a much higher price in the open market. There was an officer called the R.T.O. (rationing officer) & D.S.O. (district supply officer) who controlled and managed the supply. A friend of the family, originally from Kannauj, was D.S.O. of the Agra district. He was like family, and we called him Shukli chacha, and he and his family visited us very often. This was a very powerful position, and people tried to ingratiate themselves with him, and he controlled a lot of commodities. I remember going to Mathura (a place of pilgrimage about 40 miles away) with my aunt and Shukli chacha's wife in a Rolls-Royce car. I later learned that the car was courtesy of the royal family of Bharatpur state.

88, Civil lines circa 1989

We, like most Hindu families, were vegetarians. Strict Hindus did not eat eggs, garlic, or onion. All cooking was done with ghee (clarified butter) which was relatively expensive, as was all food. Few in North India used mustard oil for cooking; it was mostly used for body massage or as fuel for some lamps. Vegetable oil, much cheaper, was gradually getting more prevalent but was considered inferior to ghee. Most families would not admit to using it and kept it hidden from view. There were many brands in round tin containers in semi-solid hydrogenated form. 'Dalda' was the leading brand. Peanut and coconut oil was not used in our part of the country. We continued to buy whole spices and grain, like wheat, rice, gram, and lentils, in large gunny sacks at the wholesale market (mandi) in the city. This was brought home by tonga, stored, and milled at a nearby small mill (chakki) on an as-needed basis. The spices were pulverized in a stone or iron mortar and pestle (khal-morha). We also had a small round stone mill (chakki) with a wooden handle which my mother used when she wanted to use coarser grain flour. All vegetables were bought daily at the nearest vegetable market (subzi-mandi) by either the servant or one of us. A little later, vendors started hawking in our neighborhood, with the produce on flat push carts with bicycle wheels, announcing their presence by extolling the freshness and quality of their wares in colorful and loud voices.

Buying the vegetables at the mandi was an experience in itself. We bicycled to the market with sturdy home-made, rectangular, jute or cotton bags (thaila) with dual handles and a written or mental list of what Mom wanted. The market was called Ghatia, on the road past St. Peter's church. The first few shops on both sides were butchers with fresh slabs of meat hanging from hooks out front, followed by a few general merchant shops, then the vegetable vendors, till the next crossroads. Most had their vegetables spread in heaps over burlap sheets near the edge of the road. There were several small lanes leading to the vendors in the back. Water was constantly sprinkled over the vegetables to prevent them from drying out. You asked for the price of what you wanted in weight per 'sair' (about two pounds) or by bunches. After a little bargaining, and if needed, trying other vendors to compare prices and quality, the product selected was weighed on a hand-held scale and poured into your bag. If you were a regular customer, a bunch or two of greens like cilantro (dhania) or mint (pudina) would be added to your purchase-gratis. The bags were put in a wicker basket in the front of the bicycle or hung on the sides of the handlebar on the way home. Most of the time, the entire purchase would be about a rupee, about 1/80 of the present dollar. Occasionally it would be less than that by an 'anna' (one 1/16 of a rupee). So that would be our pocket money! Fruit vendors were separate and sold from carts. All fruits and vegetables were seasonal, as there was no way to preserve them. Cauliflower, cabbage, peas, carrots, potatoes, and tomatoes were winter crops, and long white radishes, pumpkins, bitter gourd (karela), and other greens were summer ones. Potatoes were more expensive in the summer, for they came from the foothills of the Himalayas. During the summer, my father would go out for his daily walk in the morning, past the Civil courts, to a small outdoors mandi that sold locally grown produce wholesale. He would get watermelon, cantaloupe, kakri (a long green vegetable of various sizes, related to the cucumber family, I think), and mangoes, and bring them in a bag or if too heavy, on a cart, and later on, on a bicycle rickshaw, He would always send some to the neighbors.

All the food was cooked from scratch. Seven days a week. I never saw my mother use a recipe or measure any ingredients. The thumb and first two fingers of her right hand- were her measuring scale. She made her own pickles, paapar, chat, murabba (preserves), and other snacks. She was an excellent cook. Going out to eat at a restaurant was not a concept.

Breakfast was either 'mathri' (small thin discs of fried bread), 'sev' (small fried chickpea-flour noodles), ladoos, or leftover parathas from dinner, with milk, in winter. Lassi (sweet yogurt drink) or freshly made fritters, any time in the morning in summer. Lunch varied between 9.30 a.m. to 2pm. depending on people's schedules. Early, if you went to work. Most places of work started around 10 a.m. Between 4 p.m. and 5 p.m. was tea and snack time, with things similar to breakfast. We drank tea only occasionally or when there was a guest. Dinner was between 8pm and 9pm and everything was made from scratch.

Lunch was 'kacha khana' (literally - partially cooked), hard to translate, but obviously cooked. This meant Roti (fluffed flat bread), rice, dal (lentil), karhi (made from chickpea flour), a dry vegetable dish, a yogurt preparation, green chutney, 'achar' (pickle) and 'paapar' (baked or fried lentil wafer). Food was cooked on a 'Choolaah' in one corner of the kitchen. This was a foot-high, horse-shoe shaped clay oven, open at the top and front, and used wood logs for fire. Things to be cooked were placed on top of that, and the degree of heat was adjusted by manipulating the small logs. Once my mother had everything organized and close to the choolaah, she would draw a line with a 'kharia' (chalk) around the area, and no one was allowed to cross that. This was probably a tradition done for sanitary purposes. The rotis were made one at a time, and we ate them fresh off the 'tava' (hot plate). The dal was served with ghee (clarified butter) on top, and the roti top was smeared with it too. We sat nearby, outside the line, on 'patras' (small, low wooden platforms. The food was served in a 'thali' (a round metal tray with an inch-high rim). Anything with liquid was served in a' katori' (a round metal container). Except for the kids, everyone ate at a different time. When my cousins were visiting, or I visited them, we ate from the same thali.

Dinner was 'pakka khana' (cooked food) again hard to translate- obviously cooked. This was cooked on a portable ‘angeethi,’ a round iron oven with an open top and a front window, side handles, and a grate in the middle. Charcoal or coke was used as fuel. The bread was paratha’ (sautéed flat bread), plain or stuffed. Several sabzis (vegetables) and condiments. There was no chalk line. There was no ‘kacha khana ' on holy festivals. In winter, mom sometimes made rotis or parathas of ‘bajra’ (millet) or ‘jowar’ (sorghum) which we ate with ‘gur’ (jaggery). Before anyone ate the food, it was offered to God. This was called’ bhog lagana’.

All utensils were made of ‘peetal’ (brass). Vessels for cooking, ‘pateeli’, were round, with a slightly narrow neck and a flared top. A pincer-like gadget, ‘sansi’ or’ sanasi,’ was used to put it on the fire and take it off. The tong to handle the roti was called ‘chimta.’

Most things were reused, repaired, or recycled, and waste was at a minimum, for things of daily living were expensive. It was practically considered a sin to throw away leftover food, which was given to beggars, the disabled- who were ubiquitous, or to stray animals. Newspapers and magazines were saved and sold to the ‘raddiwala’ (collector of discarded material), who came around and paid with metal utensils. Anything mechanical that could be was repaired. Clothes were hand-me-downs in most large families and, when worn out, used as rags or given to the poor. We had a tailor, a middle-aged Muslim man, who, for some unknown reason, called Bonton by everyone, came and altered my father's or Ravi Bhaiya's old clothes for me, sew blouses, pajamas, or other small items for the family. He used my mother's small, hand-operated, old Singer sewing machine.

Most women and young girls learned to knit, crochet, and sew. My sister knitted most of my woolen sweaters. They did this effortlessly while talking or gossiping and barely glancing at the needles. My mother made my sleeveless tank tops (banyan) and pocket-less, stringed shorts (janghia) for summer wear on her sewing machine when I was a young boy.

Agra

Agra is an ancient town situated on the banks of the Jumna (Yamuna) river in a rich, fertile, alluvial plain. It was called Agravan in ancient times. Ptolemy mentions it as Agra. Ibrahim Lodi made it his capital in 1504. It prospered when the Mughal emperor Akbar again made it his capital. He built a huge red sandstone fort on its southern bank, the Red Fort. He also built Fatehpur Sikri as a new capital on the outskirts, bordering the desert of Rajasthan. His immediate descendants continued the monument building. The large Jama- Masjid (mosque), many grand palaces, Itmad-uddaulah, and other mausoleums, of which the Taj Mahal is the most beautiful example, gardens, reservoirs, and gates. The famous Urdu poets Mirza Ghalib, Mir Taqui Mir, and Nazir were born in Agra. It became a huge commercial hub. Mandis and bazaars named after a person or the thing sold there, e.g., loha (iron) mandi, jeen-ki-mandi (bridles, stirrups, etc.), hing (asafetida), nai (barber) ki mandi and others thrived. The main bazaar started at Phoolhatti bazaar (flowers), a congested narrow street of two-storied buildings with businesses and shops. A small section of which was the 'red light district,' where women wearing heavy make-up sat in balconies, smiling and gesturing to pedestrians on the streets to come up. The bazaar continued ahead about another mile, past the Fuvara (fountain) as Johari bazaar (jeweler's market), then as Kinari bazar to the Jama Masjid (main mosque). Neighborhoods grew around them, on narrow streets and narrower intertwining lanes, forming a congested, crowded, bustling city.

The British demolished a large number of gates and monuments to make the city more manageable, consistent with their idea of modernization. They also converted some gardens into small and large parks all around the city. There was a military cantonment (army) and later an air-force base at the southern edge of the city, with an exclusive area for their residence on sprawling grounds. There were seven train stations for the two kinds of train systems. (Two each as

Agra Fort and Rajamandi, one each as City, Gadhapara, and Cantonment. With the dominance of the nearby (120 miles) Capital city of Delhi, Agra, though a large city, lost some of its importance. It remained a major tourist center, thanks to the Taj, Fort, and other monuments. It remained the premier city of the western part of the U.P. (United Provinces of Agra and Oudh). It became a very large educational center with a University that affiliated colleges as far away as Gwalior to the south, Meerut to the north, Ajmer to the west, and Kanpur to the east. The city itself had three major reputable colleges, St. John's, Agra College, and B. Rajput College, a medical and engineering college, to which students came from all over the country. It had the second-largest leather and shoe industry in North India. It was also a major center for old traditional crafts of fine and decorative stone and marble work and carpet weaving. It was renowned for its 'petha' (made from a gourd), 'gazak' (made from sesame seed) sweets, and savory 'dalmoth' (fine, tiny chickpea flour strands and dal), much imitated but never equaled elsewhere. It also had one of the few mental asylums in North India.

Like most Indian cities and towns, there was no planned pattern of growth, and the town expanded from the ancient inner city as the population increased. There were many small and large public parks (Bagh) in the outskirts which eventually got engulfed in the expansion. Baker bagh, Dayal bagh, Ram bagh, and Motilal Park come to mind.

Weather

Some of the climate was described a little bit earlier. There were five seasons. Winter, from November to the beginning of March. Spring from March to early May. Summer from May to early July, and Rainy season from July to the end of September, and a short autumn- to November.

Winter was cold by Indian standards. The temperature ranged from 32f- 70f with occasional rain, hail, and frost. The spring was sunny and mild, and the summer really hot and dry, with temps sometimes reaching 115F. At times a hot wind (Loo) would blow in the daytime and a sandstorm at night (Kali aandhi) from the nearby desert of Rajasthan, making it feel like real hell. Heat strokes were not uncommon, with an occasional death. People used umbrellas for protection, and westernized men wore khaki colored solar hats. Government office windows and doors were left open and the opening covered with thick mats of woven 'Khus' grass stems, which were periodically sprayed with water. It was surprising how much it cooled the interior. Inside were ceiling fans. The rooms were generally high ceilinged with ventilators near the ceiling to let the hot air out. Improvised cheap air-conditioning! At night people slept outside if they had the space or on flat roofs. This was because houses were either made of brick or stone, which got heated during the day and radiated it at night. Most people did not have electric fans and used hand fans of various shapes, sizes, and materials to cool themselves. The rainy season, as described earlier, was my least favorite. The schools opened, and the local book and stationery stores in the book market at Hospital Road would become crowded with students and parents (mostly the father). Autumn was short but pleasant, sliding gradually into winter.

Mail

There were post offices in large neighborhoods. The larger ones were also telegraph offices. Mail was delivered and picked up twice a day from small, red, iron mailboxes marked 'Royal Mail,' hanging from a wall all around town, and in our area, at the gate to the entrance of the Bima Company. The mailmen wore a khaki uniform. The most common form of communication was the postcard which cost 2 paisa (1/32 Rs.). Envelopes were used for more voluminous correspondence or sending small light things like a photograph. Telegrams were expensive, charged by the word, therefore short, not used often, were delivered around the clock by a special courier on a bicycle, and were received with apprehension as they often carried messages of death or serious illness.

Few people had telephones. They were mostly at larger company offices. In our area, there was only one- at the Swadeshi Bima Company office. It was a two-piece contraption. An on the base speaker and a cone-shaped earpiece attached to it by a wire to hold near your ear. To place a call, you had to call the operator and say the number you wanted, and wait to be connected. Long distance calls called trunk calls had to be booked, and the operator would call you back when the line was ready. This could be from a few minutes to several hours and was expensive.

Urban Transport

Most people easily walked distances of a mile or two. The most common form of transportation was the bicycle. Public transportation was by Tongas (horse-drawn carriages), as described earlier. You could hire the entire tonga or could pay by the seat if it was going in the direction of your destination. Fares were bargained by haggling. Cars were few, for only the wealthy could afford them. Also, they could not easily navigate the narrow and crowded inner city streets. Trucks (Lorries) were small and few. Most heavy materials were transported on mule or donkey back or by flat bullock carts, so the roads outside the city did not have much traffic. These roads were also narrow with no sidewalk, and the shoulder was just unpaved dirt.

Top picture-Ekka

Middle picture-Bullock cart

Bottom picture- Tonga

Industry

The country was overwhelmingly agricultural and rural, with little industry, which was just starting. There were cotton, jute, and wool mills. Factories were making some consumer goods like biscuits (cookies) - J.B. Mangharam, pottery- Bengal Pottery, and Gwalior Pottery. Those of shoes, utensils, cigarettes, etc., were slowly emerging. Major industrialists like Tata, Birla, Godrej, Dalmia, Dhariwal, and other manufacturers were expanding business. Most 'modern' things and nearly all machinery were imported, mainly from Britain. Razor blades, toothbrushes, cosmetics, and most gadgets were imported, hence not cheap. Electricity was very expensive and mostly powered by coal, so most household light bulbs were of low wattage- 20 or 40 watts. Street lights on the main roads were far apart and dimly lit. At night the illumination was barely the minimum for getting by. My father was very particular that the section of the house not being used should not be lit. We were reprimanded if we forgot to turn the light off when leaving a room. In the gallery of our house, we had a '0' watt light bulb to keep the inside from being totally dark at night. Higher power bulbs were available and used during functions or celebrations but were seldom in normal use by the middle class.

Currency

The currency was the Rupee or Rupiah in Hindi. It consisted of sixteen Annas. Each Anna was worth four Paisas. A Paisa was twelve Pais. Up to my grandfather's time, each Paisa was worth sixty-four Cowrie shells. I had seen cowrie shells but not as currency. The coinage was a Rupee, half a rupee (Athanni), a quarter of a rupee (Chavanni), Two annas (Duanni), one anna (Ikanni), half anna (Adhanni), pice (paisa), half paisa (Dhela), and pai. The shapes and sizes varied. Predominantly round, some square, with either a smooth or serrated edge. One variation of a paisa had a hole in the middle. The lower denominations were metal alloy. Older rupee coins were silver. All had the head of the reigning British monarch in profile on the front, except the one with the hole. Some unofficial gold coins called Ginni and Asharfi were used as presents by the wealthy. Paper currency was called 'Note.' It came in hundred, fifty, ten, five, two, and one rupee forms. Each was different in size and color, with the Monarch's face in the front. They also came in higher denominations, but I never saw any. The Indian term 'Lakh' was used officially for a hundred thousand and 'Crore' for ten million. Some larger Indian princely states had their own coins in lower denominations. The one closest to us was Gwalior. The coins were legal tender outside the state too.

Weights and Measures

Weights and measures were dual- Indian and British. The Indian and commonly used weight was the Sair (Seer in the anglicized version). It consisted of twelve 'Chatanks.' Weights came in sair, half sair (adha sair), pau (quarter sair), and two, one and half- chatank. Forty sairs was a 'Mun' (Maund in anglicized version). The smaller weight class, used mostly by jewelers, was Tola. It was made up of twelve Mashas. Each Masha was eight Rattis. Pound and ounce were known but seldom used. There were weight machines in some public places like railway platforms. Which, being manufactured in Britain, dislodged a ticket with the weight in 'stones'. Distances and length were measured in the British Mile, furlongs, yards, feet and inches, officially. The Indian 'Kos', about two miles, was used unofficially in the countryside. Tailors used 'Gaz', (about a yard) and 'Girah'. Agricultural area was measured in Acres and in the villages by 'Bigha' (about half an acre).

Families

Most Hindu and Muslim families were 'joint' families in the sense that there was a 'pater familias,' under whose tutelage lived his brothers and their families, his children, their children, and the great and, if any, great-grandchildren. So several generations lived under the same roof and ate from the same kitchen. Age was respected, obeyed, and honored at home and in society. One grew up with conviviality, tolerance, unity, and the enormous love and support which came with it. There was some loss of independence, but traditionally it was not sought, as one grew up seeing a similar situation among one's peers. It was not that differences did not occur, but tolerance, and self-control, imbued from birth, was part of the glue that kept the family together. Sometimes families did split, but often it was a matter of social shame in the community, and rare. First cousins, especially on the father's side, were treated as and called brother or sister, which at times caused a little confusion to outsiders. All this started to erode gradually as people became mobile due to modernization, for mobility was forced by jobs, business opportunities, and other factors. Our family split in 1928 as my father was accepted to head the newly opened Hindi department at St. John's College in Agra, though they remained a joint family as he was the sole family wage earner. More on that later.

Ravi, my uncle's son, joined the family at Agra in 1946 to continue his education, after completing high school at Kannauj. He was admitted to St. John's College in what was called 'Intermediate,' the first two years of the bachelor's program. He was eight years older than me. I began to idolize him as an older brother, and he became Ravi Bhaiya (brother

Ravi). My grandparents would come from Kannauj, singly or together, and stay till they became homesick and went back. In the three houses in the immediate neighborhood, we had enough kids to play cricket in the lane behind our house or the larger vacant lot in front of the Bima Company building. There were also lots of girls in the neighborhood for my sister to socialize with.

Language

The language we spoke in the city was Hindi. Some called it Hindustani (Indian). The standard spoken and written form was called 'Khari Boli.' But there were many dialects, scores of them. It seemed the dialect changed every 40-50 miles. So much so that what was spoken in the eastern part of our province (U.P.) was practically unintelligible in the western part. People used a lot of similes, sayings, proverbs, and aphorisms, which made the speech very colorful and lively. Terms like 'Dur ke dhol suhavane' (drums sound better when afar). 'Oonchi dukaan pheeka pakwan' (a showy shop has insipid fare).' Thotha chana baje ghana' (empty vessels make a lot of noise). 'Aaj maray kal dusra din' (dead today, tomorrow's another day). 'Andhon mein kana raja' (among the blind, one-eyed man is king).And many more. The most astounding and descriptive one was in a conversation I overheard on a bus in Bhopal. A passenger was describing the degree of closeness between two friends with 'Woh ek gand say hagtay hain' (they shit from the same asshole). Urdu, a variant of Hindi with more Persian and Arabic words, was spoken by upper-class Muslims and some Hindus. Urdu was written in a modified script of Persian, from right to left. And Hindi in the Devanagari script from left to right. Just as Hindi acquired Persian and Arabic words over the years from rulers using Persian, English started to creep up in conversational Hindi, with English words substituting Hindi ones. English was spoken in an Indianized version by British-educated people, often translating their Hindi thoughts literally. *In Hindi/Urdu, an adjective is repeated for emphasis, e.g.,' uske pas achi achi cheezain hain' would become 'he has nice nice things.' 'Only then' would become 'then only.' Written English conformed to the usual form but continued to use terms long abandoned in other English-speaking countries.* The use of words and phrases like 'pray,' 'your most obedient servant,' and 'yours faithfully' continued. Many English words were used in Hindi and dialects in their Indian incarnation. Signal down became singal dawn. Collector-kallatar, Ma'm (madam) saheb-mem saheb. Lord saheb- laat saheb. Pliers-plas. Driver-delaiver. Lantern-laltain, bottle-'botal' And lots more.

I spoke English at school, Hindi socially, and the Kannauj dialect of Hindi at home. My mother and grandmother only spoke dialect. It was understood by everyone but probably sounded funny to them. It was different from the dialect spoken around Agra- (Brij bhasha).

Entertainment

Public entertainments were movie houses (cinemas), sports events such as inter-collegiate matches in cricket, football (soccer), and hockey (field hockey), along with fairs, an occasional circus, and itinerant showmen with trained animals. Annually there was Ram Lila, an enactment of the story of Lord Rama for about ten or more days in the fall, culminating on Dussehra day. Nearly every city and the town had designated grounds for this. In Agra, it was across from the Red Fort. A major episode of the story would be enacted every evening. It was like a fair every day, with Indian fast food, toy vendors, and rides. There were two main episodes. One was the wedding of Lord Rama, when a large procession, with marching bands, elephants, and horses decorated with colorful costumes and tinkling bells, formed the wedding party passing through the main bazaar in the evening. The riders threw coins, toys, and candy to the huge crowds lined on both sides of the route. The second was the killing of the demon Ravana, an ogre with ten heads, followed by the ceremonial burning of his effigy.

A dying form of village entertainment was the Nautanki. This was a touring group that held music/dance dramas based on popular folk tales in larger villages. It had male and female artists, bright propane lights, and loud music- all a rare and welcome diversion from the daily grind. Nagaara (a large drum), played by sticks, was its hallmark and could be heard over a quarter mile away at night.

The snake charmers, famed and renowned internationally, an exotic symbol of India in colonial times, need a little elaboration. These were professionals from whom the art was passed down in the family for generations. They made their rounds in a family group with snakes in a few wicker baskets covered by cloth sheets and played on a 'Been' (a flute made out of a gourd). They carried a variety of snakes, the most popular being the cobra. Once the price of the show was settled, they would take out the snake and start playing the 'been,' and the snake would gradually rise, spread its hood and undulate in front of the snake charmers' 'been.' It was quite a captivating and mesmerizing spectacle with people, especially children, forming a circle around the show at a 'safe' distance, influenced by the primeval fear of snakes. For it was taught from an early age that all snakes were poisonous, so most Indians grew up with this misconception and in fear of all snakes.

Similarly, a group with trained Rhesus monkeys would enact a drama of a wife getting angry at her husband and leaving him, and he would go to her to ask her to come back. It was fascinating. In another group, there was a show where a small Indian black bear would dance to the playing of a small hour-glass shaped, hand-held drum (damru).

The other means of entertainment were gramophones, radio, movies, and local sports events. Gramophones were wound up by a crank, and a cone-shaped top would emit the sound. Record albums were expensive, and not many people owned the system. Radios, too, were not very common due to the expense and the need for electricity. You needed a license to own one. They were, like most mechanicals, imported. There were two broadcast frequencies, medium and short waves, and they required an elaborate outside antenna for reception. The closest radio station was Delhi, about 120 miles away. It had quite a variety of programs. Literary discussions, classical Indian music, information for farmers, interviews with prominent people, and other serious matters. News in English and Hindi was broadcast several times a day. On Sunday mornings, there would be a program for children, which was very entertaining. The reception and sound quality depended on the weather and the working of the antenna. As few small towns and villages were electrified, battery-powered radios were used by the few who could afford them, with friends gathering around it at the time of news or a popular broadcast.

Cricket was wildly popular among the urbanized. There were 'Test' matches lasting five days, played in major cities, with visiting teams like M.C.C., West Indies, Australia, Pakistan, and others, which were broadcast by a running commentary and a play-by-play description on All India radio. Young people would be glued to the radio, and some even skipped classes. Soccer (football) and hockey (field hockey) though less popular, also had large followings with national tournaments. Dhyan Chand, a hockey legend, was still remembered with awe. Cricket stars were nearly as popular as film stars. Names like Cowdry, Hutton, and Pataudi of the UK. Merchant, Manjeraker, Manked, Mushtaque Ali, Hazare, and Gupte Phadkar of India, Worrall, and Weeks of the West Indies are still fresh in my memory. Also, the legends of old like Ranji and Bradman. I can recall the play-by-play radio commentary by 'Vizzy.'

Hobbies were limited to the middle and upper classes. A few friends and I collected stamps, and I had a respectable collection in my album. It was fun trading them with friends.

Some collected coins, I did too, but mine was relatively small.

Cinema (Movies)

The most popular and rapidly developing form of entertainment was the movies- or cinema as it was popularly called, also limited to electrified places. There were several movie houses distributed around town. They were all called 'talkies' and 'bi-scope' by the older generation. The ones I remember are Roxy, Chitra, Taj, Bharat, and Krishna in the city and Nand and Imperial in the cantonment area. Imperial only showed English-language movies. There were three shows each day. 3p.m. to 6pm. was a matinee, 6 p.m. to 9 p.m. first show, and 9p.m to 12pm second show. In larger cities, movie houses were spectacular buildings, inside and out.

Most movies were boilerplate comedies and a few tragedies. Comedies were around the formula of a boy and girl falling in love, and after many hurdles, love triumphed. Each movie started with 'God save the king' before Indian independence. Later it started with a brief government-made documentary called a news-reel, of a current natural disaster, like flooding or a visit by a foreign dignitary, followed by a copy of the certification from the censor board for films and a few trailers of forthcoming attractions. There were six to ten songs and dance numbers, and it was about two and a half to three hours long. There was an Interval (intermission) of five to ten minutes in the middle. This was marked with a sale of songbooks of the film, tea, snacks, and scalp massage (champi). There were also some religious films based on Hindu mythology. A small genre was 'stunt' films like Ustad (Master) Pedro and Hunterwali (woman with a whip).Performers were type casted.

Initially, the movie industry was in Calcutta but then moved to Bombay. Since Hindi was the most widely spoken and understood language, most movies were in Hindi. Due to the popularity of their music and performers, they also became popular in non-Hindi-speaking areas and inadvertently helped spread Hindi all over India. There were also small regional language industries in Bengal and the South. Western films, mostly Hollywood, and some British, were shown in theaters in Calcutta and Bombay as part of their world premiere and in other large cities. Popular actors were Gregory Peck, Cary Grant, Robert Taylor, Stewart Granger, Kirk Douglas, James Stewart, Dean Martin, Jerry Lewis, Ingrid Bergman, Rita Hayworth, Marilyn Monroe, Grace Kelly, and Audrey Hepburn.

There were a select few Indian leading men and women as actors who were typecast in roles of hero (leading man), the heroine (leading lady), villain, mother, funnyman, and dancer. Sehgal, Prithviraj, Ashok Kumar, Sohrab Modi, Yakub, Shyam, Karan Dewan, Moti Lal, Dilip Kumar. Bharat Bhushan, Raj Kapoor, and Dev Anand, as leading men, in descending order of seniority, come to mind. Similarly, Suraiya, Meena Kumari, Madhubala, Bina Rai, Geeta Bali, and Nargis, in leading ladies. Jeevan and Pran as villains. Durga Khote as a widowed mother, and Gope, Yakub, Mukri, Agha, and Johnny Walker as comics. Most of these names were stage names. Very few of the actors could sing, so songs were dubbed- called play-back. Popular male singers were Sehgal, Mohammad Rafi, Mukesh, Talat Mahmood, Manna Dey, Hemant Kumar, and Kishor Kumar. Female singers included Noor Jehan, Shamshad Begum, Lata Mangeshkar, Asha Bhonsle, and Geeta Dutt. Film music rapidly evolved from semi-classic Indian to western, both in instruments and rhythm. Stories and music were freely plagiarized from Hollywood. There were magazines like Film India and Filmfare and Screen devoted solely to the industry. Soon the industry became the world's largest. Films were exported worldwide to the Indian diaspora and were also popular in Southeast Asia, the middle-east and the Soviet Union. There was a tiny Jewish community in Bombay, and they contributed to Indian cinema. The dancer Helen and actor David come to mind.

As the major source of popular entertainment, film music became popular, though initially shunned by the nationalized government-controlled All India Radio. Radio Ceylon, a private offshore station playing Indian music in the western format all day long, became wildly popular among the young. Its Binaca Geetmala (film songs) became a craze. The bigger pan shops and some smaller restaurants had film music blaring nonstop from a small radio.

Young people still were not able to listen to or sing love-songs openly as society still considered it to be unacceptable. Neither was what was depicted in the movies, a reflection of society. Nonetheless, the young, especially men, imitated the hairstyles, fashions, and mannerisms of their film idols as much as possible. The upturned shirt collar and the partially rolled trouser legs. A few even ran away from home to Bombay, the Hollywood of India, to try to become actors. It became so frequent that ads like 'Please come home, your Mother has not eaten since you left. All will be forgiven,' could be seen in national newspapers. Bombay Police had a special squad to intercept runaways at its railway stations.

Music

Indian classical music, instrumental and vocal, developed over thousands of years, was the sole means of entertainment of the elite before colonization, patronized by the princely states and wealthy landlords, as was poetry. With the decline of these patrons, both fell on hard times. Instrumental and vocal music was saved by All India Radio by patronizing the artists. Poets, Hindi and Urdu, started moving to the film industry to write screen -plays and lyrics for them. Hence the high quality of the lyrics of earlier films. Film music adapted and added on Western popular rhythm and beat and Western instruments.

Others

Rarely a circus would come to town and be held at the Ram Lila grounds. Circuses were rather small but had the attraction of elephants, tigers, horses, lions, clowns, trapeze artists, and motorcycle pits. More on that later. Inter-school and collegiate sports were free, open to the public, and well attended.

Major Festivals

The Hindu calendar is a soli-lunar system with 12 months. There is something of religious importance nearly every day, and it is too involved to explain. Several days in a month were celebrated with fasts of different kinds. Nothing at all, to- just water, just fruit or Kootoo (a grain). There were scores of minor festivals. Major festivals were Vaisakhi, Basant, Janmashtami, Holi, Dushehra, Diwali, and Eid for the Muslims and Christmas for Christians.

Basant was in spring when the fields turned yellow with mustard flowers. Everyone wore at least one piece of clothing, which was yellow. Vaisakhi was the first month of the calendar, also in spring. Dussehra was the burning of the effigy of Ravana, symbolizing the triumph of good over evil and the end of Ram Lila. Among Khatris (my caste), there was 'Astra puja' or worship of any weapon, e.g., a knife (most commonly) or a gun. Diwali is described later.

Holi was in the spring and was celebrated on a full moon, predawn, by lighting a pyre of wood, symbolic of an ancient legend. Every neighborhood had a designated place for it. Some bought firewood. We went around the neighboring hills trying to cut dead branches from bushes, collecting sticks, raiding anything wooden anywhere, and piling it on the pyre. People protected and brought in their wooden furniture and belongings from outside since it was fair game. Raiding others' pyre was not uncommon. Some toasted bunches of gram pods- 'boot,' in the fire. Dousing each other with colored water and powder (gulal) started in the morning. It was a joyous occasion. Everyone tried to wear old but white clothes to highlight the colors. We would fill up buckets with colored water and spray each other and passers-by on the road using long metal sprayers (pichkari). Apply gulal on faces. Days earlier, we would make small round wax containers in metal forms (kumkuma), fill them with colored water, seal them, and use them as hand grenades exploding color on people. All this was called playing Holi. People would gather and visit neighbors in a group to play Holi. Grownups would embrace each other, and all previous enmity was forgotten, and were served some refreshments and 'Thandai' (described earlier). Some added a little bhang to it. It ended about noon when everyone took a bath and tried to scrub off the colors from their body. Sometimes it took days to do that.

Janmashtami was the birthday of Lord Krishna, celebrated at midnight, the time of his birth. My mother fasted (nothing by mouth) and prepared a feast and many sweets, including my favorite- gond-ki-katli (a sweet made with gum). I remember fasting once or twice. People set up elaborate displays of Lord Krishna's birth. He was born in prison and then smuggled out and transported across the Jumna River on a sifter, during a fierce storm, in Mathura.

There were a large number of Hindu temples devoted to God in the form of different deities all over town and the outskirts. Each with its devout followers. Our family was partial to Mankameshwar devoted to Lord Shiva. It is in the middle of the congested inner city and is accessible by going through a very narrow lane.

Worship

Most Hindu families had a small area or a room for Puja (worship) at home. Pictures and idols and incarnations were kept there. Going to the temple was as desired. Akhand Ramayan Path (continuous recitation of the story of Rama) was pretty common, especially in our family. This was done at home, thanking God for the fulfillment of a wish. It consisted of a 24-hour uninterrupted recitation of the Ramayana written in verse by the poet Tulsi Das in the sixteenth century. Members of the family, neighbors, and friends took turns in an uninterrupted reading.

Satyanarayan Katha was a religious recitation by the family priest at home, again with family and friends as thanks for a fulfilled wish. This was of about an hour's duration.

Bhajan and Kirtan were devotional songs sung individually or in chorus, accompanied by manjeera (small cymbals), harmonium, and dholak (a short two-sided drum). At the end of each of these, Prasad (offering) was distributed in donas (dry leaf containers). Commonly, Panjeeri (roasted, sweet, wheat flour), barfi or ladoo, and charanamrit (sweetened milk with nuts in it).

Growing up in a Hindu family, I knew a little more about it and its mythology than about the other religions, though I was exposed to them. I knew about Roman Catholicism and Protestantism from my school environment. Christmas and Easter were not much known or celebrated outside the Indian Christian and Anglo-Indian communities, which were tiny. Muslim festivals, especially Eid, were well known because of the larger communities and interactions with them. There was a large Idgah (place for prayers on Eid) on the outskirts of town where the worship and celebrations took place. People dressed up and wore new clothes. It was frequent for Muslims to share sweets with their Hindu friends on the day. Muharram, a Shia Muslim holiday, was a procession of mourning described earlier. There were also some fairs (Urs) held at the tombs (dargah) of revered Muslim holy men (pirs). There were mosques in Muslim neighborhoods with the Muezzin (announcer) calling the faithful for prayer five times a day.

Jains (followers of Jainism) were indistinguishable from Hindus in name and dress. They were exclusively traders by profession, and there were frequent intermarriages with Hindus. Hindus did not consider them different. They were strictly non-violent and would not kill any living thing. One hallmark of the Jains was that they ate dinner before dark, ostensibly to prevent eating any insect or living thing accidentally in the food, in poor light. Some even went around placing wheat flour around ants' nests.

Sikhs were distinguishable by their turbans, beards, and iron wrist bangles (Choora). They had Hindu first names followed by Singh. Many also had Hindu last names. They were also a tiny minority till after the partition of India when many moved east and settled in North Indian towns. Hindus treated them as fellow religionists.

Parsis were a small but prosperous community that had settled mostly in west-central India after fleeing from Islamic persecution over a thousand years ago, from Iran. . They were in important professions, industries and trades. They had ancient Persian first names. The families in Agra that I knew were Prof. Dorrab and Dr. Mrs. Barucha, a female pediatrician.

There were a few very ancient Jewish settlements in south India and a larger one in Bombay. Some of them were in films. David and Helen, as mentioned earlier. My only contact with them was with my school classmate for two years, David Reuben. The family moved away, and I did not know much about them.

Charitable Institutions

Most large towns and cities had shelters for orphans (anathalaya) and widows (widhwa ashram) where free boarding and lodging and training in some form of arts and craft was offered. Some wealthy people maintained water stations (pyau) all over town, where a person sitting on a high platform poured water from a metal container with a spout (gangasagar) to the thirsty person who formed a cup to his mouth with one or both his palms (chullu) to drink.

My Early Years

At the end of the school year, in second standard, I got my report card- actually a paper with subjects and marks earned out of a hundred in each, with a brief remark from the teacher and her and the headmaster's signature at the bottom. I came first in my class. When I handed my report to my father, he seemed happy, and so were my mother, sister, and Ravi Bhaiya. But there was no great fuss made over that. It was arbitrarily decided, I think by my father, that I was 'weak' in arithmetic, so a tutor was arranged who would come in the evening for an hour and teach me arithmetic and Hindi. Hindi, I presumed, because it was still not taught at the school. I did not particularly care for this arrangement, for it interfered with my playtime with friends. But I had no choice. Six days a week, except for major holidays.

In the summer, school hours were from 7 a.m. to noon, and the classes were shorter, with a short break midmorning. The first period was catechism- but non-Christians were excused and were allowed to stay and study in the study hall. For the rest of the year, each period was about 40 minutes. In the evening, there was mandatory participation in sports. It was football (soccer) from August-September, field hockey till November, then cricket till the end of the school year and spring. The sport started at about 4.30 p.m. and lasted an hour. Teams were made of similar age groups. Mr. Eastwood, one of the teachers, played hockey and football with us. Sometimes we would have matches with St. George's across town. There was no interaction with other schools in the city. The athletic meet was held once a year and had the usual jumps, throws, and races. We did not have long-distance races. I played all the sports but was not outstanding in any. That made me more competitive.

I was skinny and short for my age. My father had me checked by Dr. Bagchi and a few others from the large circle of his physician friends. These were just physical exams. The result was that I was put on different 'tonics.' These were concoctions of vitamins and alcohol, and most of them tasted awful. Also, a raw egg stirred in milk was forced on me in winter as 'good nutrition' as part of breakfast. I hated the slimy texture and strange taste and always gagged and nearly vomited when forced to drink it. Why in winter only? This was because there was a belief about a particular food and its effect. Some foods like eggs and meat were considered "hot,' and were winter food. Milk products like yogurt were 'cooling,' hence only appropriate for summer. Another awful thing was to have to drink cod liver oil. It vied with the egg and milk preparation in my hatred of my health boosters. There was no subtlety in dealing with children's sensibilities. I was frequently referred to as 'small for my age,' 'skinny,' and even 'tubercular.' Maybe I was too sensitive, but I did not like to be called any of that. Had anyone stopped to consider that a child of a 5' 5" father and a 4' 8" mother is not going to be a giant, I would have been spared much of the assault on my taste buds and hurtful anguish. The intentions were probably good, but their execution was insensitive. Ever since then, I resolved to do everything other kids my age did, and if possible, better than them. I started doing push-ups and sit-ups in private and tried to eat more. But I still remained skinny.

The Country of My Childhood

At the time of Independence, there were 17 provinces in British India and 562 princely states of varying sizes, from a few villages to larger than some countries, and were considered Independent except for being under British suzerainty. The princely states were given a choice to join Pakistan or India or be independent at the time of Indian Independence. Later, this created a big mess.

Villages and Small towns

Over eighty percent of the country was rural and predominantly agricultural. Poverty, malnutrition, poor sanitation, and their attending sequelae were widespread. Agriculture was primitive, using bullock-drawn plows and human and animal waste as fertilizer. Irrigation was poor, mostly dependent on, and at the mercy of nature. All this added up to give meager yields. Subsistence farming as tenant farmers on small fields added to the woe, despite the fertile land. Food grain was imported. I remember American wheat being sold in the bazaar under the American PL30 loan program, and most people did not like it as it was reddish brown in contrast to the local light brown and tasted 'different.'

Infectious diseases and epidemics like cholera, typhoid, smallpox, tuberculosis, leprosy, trachoma, infant and maternal mortality took a heavy toll on health, productivity, and longevity. The average life span was under fifty years. Sixty was considered old. Electrification and municipal water supply were limited to cities and larger towns. Famines were a recent memory.

The villages were usually a collection of mud huts with thatched roofs, a communal well, and a pond or two surrounded by fields and orchards. Cow dung was used as plaster for the huts. It was dried in the form of discs on the roof or the side of the hut and used as fuel for cooking. It was also the main fertilizer. Cows, water buffalos, goats, and sheep were the source of milk. They were led outside the village to graze on the fallow fields, or wherever grass grew, by children or women in the morning, and returned at sunset.

The yield of milk was low due to poor nutrition and inbreeding. The open fields were used as toilets. Often the village harbored just one caste or community, or religion. Occasionally there would be a brick house or two signifying the owner's affluence. The central part of the village would have a large tree with a paved platform for gatherings like panchayat or storytelling. A panchayat was an ancient system where a grievance was settled by five mutually agreed upon elders after hearing out both sides. Entertainment was sitting around a fire on the ground or on cots (charpais) and listening to someone sing old folk songs or tales like Ala-Udal or attending village fairs. Some fairs were just about the sale of a particular domestic animal. Horses, cows, bullocks, camels, sheep, or goats.

The villagers were mostly simple illiterate folk, reconciled to their way of life and followed traditions passed on for centuries. Though simple, they were not unintelligent. Schools were opening for education in larger villages, and their children, initially only boys, started getting a basic education. Their mode of transport was mostly by foot-barefoot, and they could walk on most rough surfaces with ease as they developed thick calluses on their soles. They could and did carry surprisingly heavy bundles on their heads. Nearly all carried a lathi (bamboo staff) perched on one shoulder. They wore lace- less leather shoes (chamraudha), which they sometimes carried dangling at the end of the lathi (staff) on the shoulder, and would put them on at the approach of their destination. Paved roads were few and narrow. Most were rutted dirt roads. The main mode of transportation was the bullock cart. This was a long, flat platform, narrower in the front, made of wooden boards, and had two large wooden wheels. The front end was yoked to one or a pair of bullocks with bells tied to their necks. A few had arched canvas covers. This was used to transport people and produce. A little later, bicycles came into use, where the paths and roads were ride-able. Most traveled with a lota (a small round metal vessel) and dor (cotton string) and Sattu (parched powdered grain) tied at one end of an Angocha (long thin towel with a red print) when traveling. This enabled them to have an instant meal and water when they stopped for rest near a well or stream.

Small towns had brick-and-mortar houses, paved roads, small bazaars or mandis, and public institutions like courts, Thana (police station), post offices, schools, municipalities, temples, mosques, and Ram Lila grounds. They were smaller and rougher versions of a city. Some were even district headquarters and were electrified

My father decided that I should learn to play a musical instrument. Tabla was selected. This was a pair of drums played with fingers and the heel of the palm. An 'Ustad' (an accomplished teacher) came to teach me twice a week. I practiced hard every day but soon realized that aside from becoming a journeyman player, I did not have what it takes to be an accomplished player. I kept at it doggedly. Somehow, about a year later, the lessons stopped, but I continued to practice what I had learned. It did not go beyond that and soon tapered off.

Ravi Bhaiya would let me see his anatomy books and the various bones he studied. He was a good 'slow bowler' in cricket and played with our neighborhood kids in the mornings and on weekends and holidays. He wanted and was given a motorbike, which was a big deal, so he now rode that instead of a bicycle to college. I remember the make-Norton, for I used to clean it for him and get rewarded with a ride or a few pice. His room was the one in the back, with a verandah. My sister had a tiny room on the south side. I kept my books and toys in the room up front, which was the official but not used dining room, pretending it was my room. I was tidy and kept everything in order. I remember my shoes being black lace-ups called 'Naughty boy.' I think they were called that, for they were scuff-proof and practically indestructible. Bata Shoe Company was the only major national brand, and I think they made them. Bata was also the only one who made canvas shoes for sports. These came in ocher and white colors, and the price always ended in '99', e.g., Rs. 8.99, 12.99, and the like.

My father had changed some more. No more western suites and ties and tennis at the staff club. He started wearing Khadi (clothing made from homespun material). Dhoti and kurta at home and pants and bush-shirt to college. A bush shirt was a box-shaped shirt, open front, buttons, tail-less, with a breast pocket and a patch pocket on each lower side, worn untucked over pants. He wore canvas shoes with rubber tire soles called 'go-rakshak' (cow savers). He also wore a Gandhi Cap instead of a solar hat. He ate bland food, which my mother had to cook separately for him. He started to go for early morning and post-prandial evening walks with a walking stick. I do not know what brought on this change.

We still had a stream of visitors all day long except when he was at college. These ranged from his students, friends, acquaintances, and strangers who called without advance notice. Most were entertained with tea and snacks, which my mother had to produce on demand. She was always prepared. At least once a month, we had overnight guests who were lodged in the drawing room. The reason was that staying at a hotel was very unusual, and there were not many of them. So when one traveled to another city, one stayed with a relative, friend, or friend of a friend. It was customary to bring your own bedding in a 'hold-all'. This was a canvas, leather-enhanced contraption which could be rolled into a round bundle and carried all essential items needed for travel. If there was no one available to stay with, then there were community hostels called 'dharamshalas.' Nearly every town had them. They were built by a community or caste and lodged people for a few days, gratis or at a very minimal rate or a donation. Sometimes there was a kitchen to cook your own food.

Padam chacha had become part of the family. He would bicycle over in the evening and intermix with the family, have dinner with us and leave around 9 p.m. In the winter, my father would insist he leave earlier due to the cold and the desolateness of the road, as hardly anyone was out after sunset. He would accompany my father on most shopping trips and take part in all family discussions. He had done his Masters in Philosophy from St. John's College and had earned his bachelor's degree in Law (L.L.B.) by attending evening courses at Agra College while working at the C.O.D. (central ordnance depot) at the cantonment section of the city, about five miles away. He lived in the city not far from where we had lived. He loved politics and discussions and had long discussions and arguments with our family members and friends. He was an avid reader of the daily

English newspaper we got. He read it practically from the front to the last page. He was very knowledgeable and had firm inflexible opinions vehemently expressed. To us, it was amusing to get him involved in an argument, and sometimes people did it just to see his vehemence. He was honest, principled, and frank. My father had a habit of having his feet and lower legs massaged, and anyone available and willing was lured into doing it. The servant, kids in the family, neighborhood kids, and some of his devoted students. The trick was to get the massager involved in a conversation, so he got distracted from the chore. This strange habit seemed to run in the family. I saw my grandfather, uncle, and even Ravi Bhaiya do it. Padam chacha was his long time massager. They had endless conversations during the massage. My father's euphemism for the massage was 'desh seva' (service to the country). I don't know how that came about.

Nemi chacha, a contemporary of Padam chacha, developed lung tuberculosis and could not continue his studies. Since there was no medicine to treat it, he was advised to have the affected lung removed. My father took him to Almorha, in the foothills of the Himalayas, where there was a TB hospital, and the surgeon was a friend of his. After recouping from a successful lung removal there, Nemi chacha moved to Delhi. After that, we saw him only periodically.

My father bought a strip of land on the left side of the house and built a small shed next to the kitchen and another room next to it with its door opening on the back lane. He also built a long car garage in front, on the left, leaving the back courtyard connected to the front lawn by a small doorway. The shed had an asbestos roof. He also bought a cow which was kept there and taken care of by a cowherd. My mother now had pure unadulterated milk and started to make her own fresh butter and buttermilk. The garage was rented to Paliwalji's (a friend and neighbor) brother, who parked his long American Packard with 'fins' there. This was exciting to us kids as it looked about twice the length of other cars. The room was used as a servant's room.

The courtyard had a Kachnar (mountain ebony) tree whose flowers were spectacular and were used to make a stew. We also had a grapefruit tree, and grape juice was sometimes used as a substitute for lemon juice. On the front lawn, toward the boundary wall, there was a guava tree. We got a few fruits from it if the parrots spared some. My father tried to maintain the postage-stamp-sized lawn by watering it with a hose attached to the tap (faucet) we had near the garage. In the winter, we would sit in it to sun ourselves, including mother, who favored the back verandah. We planted some flowers at the edges with mixed success but always had some in flower pots on the front steps. Along the boundary wall was a continuous line of high bougainvillea bushes. Just outside the gate was a scrawny Sheeshum tree.

Fourth Standard

I was now in the fourth standard. The class teacher was Mr. Geyer. He was affable, mild-mannered, Anglo-Indian, and wore thick rimless glasses. He also led fourth through the eighth standard in calisthenics, in front of the school building, during the mid-morning gym period. I made more friends at school. Reggie Graham, the younger of the Graham brothers, and Ronald of the several Smiths, who were Indian Christians and lived near the school in the Ghatia area. Our classes were very small, and I think we were about fifteen in our class. The Class teacher taught all the subjects. We were still doing arithmetic using the British currency system and studying British history from books published in Britain. This would soon change.

When there was a disciplinary or other problem in class, which was rare, the culprit was told to get out. This meant standing in the veranda just outside the class entrance. The headmaster made rounds walking in the verandas around the classrooms two or three times a day. He would stop, ask the teacher what the problem was and decide on the punishment. This varied in severity. For mild infractions, you got a talking-to and made to apologize to the teacher. For a higher level, there was caning. The headmaster took you to his office and asked you to bend over, and you got caned on your bottom, from two to many more strikes, again, depending on the severity of the infraction as judged by him. Some frequent offenders, anticipating caning, wore 'double pants' (two shorts) to lessen the pain. We did not start wearing long pants till the eighth or ninth standard. The other punishment was 'to go kneel under the bell'. This was for, obviously, a higher infraction. The duration was-the rest of the class period or for a set period of time. This was not only painful, having to kneel on a hard sandstone surface on bare knees, but also to be seen by other students during recess. No communication was allowed between the punished and the gawkers. The next higher punishment was 'public caning'. This was in front of the entire assembled school. I think I saw that only once when I had just joined the school. The highest level of punishment was 'rustication,' being expelled from school. This happened once during my stay. I knew who it was but did not know the reason. Most of the punishments were meted out to the boarders as there were fewer day scholars, and they were not prone to getting in trouble. I never suffered from these, nor did my friends.

We had two exams in the academic year, 'half-year' and 'final.' I came first in my class in both. The marking system was 'A' for the top, 'C' for intermediate, 'P' for pass and 'F' for fail. The actual marks out of a hundred were written on the results sheet, but I do not remember what the differentiating marks for the grades were. My worst subject was drawing. I got 'A's in everything but just scraped through in it. I tried very hard to draw and eventually learned how to, but I still was not very good at it.

In my school system, we got a month's vacation after exams in mid-December. We also had a summer vacation from mid-May to mid-June. During my winter vacation, most of my neighborhood friends were in school, so it was a bit lonely in the daytime. I filled this time up by reading. My father had a large collection of books, mostly in Hindi but some in English too. I read the newspapers, and that got me interested in politics and the news. We used to get a local Hindi paper called Amar Ujala and a national English daily called the Indian Express. It had both national and international news. We also got an English language weekly called Shankar's weekly. It was full of political cartoons pertaining to national and international events, drawn by the famous cartoonist Shankar and a great group of other Indian cartoonists like Lakshman. It also had short articles of political satire. For some time, we also got the Illustrated Weekly of India. This was the size of the American Life magazine, and had a lot of pictures and short articles and stories. We also got four other Hindi magazines-Manohar Kahanian (pleasant stories), a monthly of short stories, and Bal Sakha (Children's friend) - a monthly for children. Sarita

(Stream), a monthly, the size of a skinny book, with varied content. Kalyan (Benediction) a copiously illustrated religious magazine on devotion and Hindu mythology, mostly for my mother, who was its avid reader. Bal Sakha stopped when I was twelve years old. In Hewett Park, the one near my school, there was a library called John's Public Library. It was a beautiful, yellow building with a tower at one end. The building was actually a large hall with lots of large glass windows. It had most of the Indian newspapers and magazines in Hindi, Urdu, and English and a large collection of books. I used to walk there and look at them. I did not become a member, so I could not check out any books. Exposure to all these, with time on my hands, awakened and nurtured my interest in literature, politics, and current events, Indian and foreign. Sometimes my father would bring some books for me to read from St. John's College library. I remember reading Dickens- Pickwick Papers and Jeeves series by P.G. Wodehouse, among many others

I also went to watch inter-collegiate cricket matches. The local medical college held annual athletic and sports events in a field below the boy's hostel. I went to see these every year. So I became familiar with the names and faces of some of the players and athletes. I remember a hulking man who was the athletic champion for several years, with the last name Seth. Ravi Bhaiya played cricket as a slow bowler, and I enjoyed watching and cheering for him. I attended their annual variety show, which was always very enjoyable.

Summer Vacations and Kannauj

Every summer, my mother, sister, and I would go to Kannauj, the family seat, for a month-long vacation. I looked forward to it for many reasons. It involved train travel and a chance to be with my cousins. Any change from the normal routine was rare, therefore welcome and exciting. Train travel was a real adventure, or so it seemed to me. Kannauj was about 120 miles to the north east on the banks of the historic and mighty Ganga River. It took us about 18 hours to get there.

My mother would pack puris (fried flat bread), sookhe aloo (sautéed potatoes), mango pickle, baysan laddoos (round sweets made of chickpea flour, sugar and ghee) and mathri (a small, deep-fried, layered, circular bread), packed in steel containers called 'catordan,' tied pyramid fashion in a cloth bundle called 'potli' Water was carried in a 'surahi' (described earlier). Our clothes would be packed in a steel trunk with a padlock. The rest, bedding, slippers, and other miscellaneous items were packed in a canvas hold-all, rolled, and tied with leather straps.

A couple of hours (or more) before train departure time, the servant or I would go to the tonga stand near Wazirpur and hire a tonga. My father renegotiated the fare and the luggage loaded, and off we went to the train station called 'City Station', about a mile and a half away. An orange-shirted coolie (porter) would then carry the luggage on his head and slung from his shoulders to the platform. We followed, while my father went to the ticket window to buy our tickets. The coolie asked for the class we were traveling by and placed the luggage near the edge of the platform. If there was still some time for the train to come he would leave and come back just before its arrival.

There were four classes of travel. First-class was a smaller car (compartment) with upholstered and relatively luxurious appointments, including a western-style toilet. For a while, there was a small car called 'servant' attached to a few first-class cars for the servants of the travelers (mostly European), for a few years after independence, on mail trains. The second class was a slightly less luxurious version of the first class. The Intermediate class was a large car with un-upholstered bench seats. The third class had long wooden seats that were longer than the inter-class. Each car (compartment) was separate and attached to the others on the outside. They had adjustable glass windows except for the third class, which sometimes had bars. The seats were arranged lengthwise on both sides and in the middle. There were luggage racks above. Near the ceiling, in the middle of each car, was a transverse metal chain, about a foot long, on both sides., over which was printed in red- 'EMERGENCY' in English, and a warning of a fine of Rs. 50 if used otherwise. This was to stop the train in case of an emergency, which was undefined. Outside each compartment, near the entryway, there was a sign indicating the class in Roman numerals for each class and INTER for intermediate.

There were two main gauges for railway tracks. Bari (larger) line and choti (small) line. The latter was also called meter gauge. The railways were run by private companies, and there were many. E.I.R. (East India railway), G.I.P. (great Indian peninsular), B.B. & C.I. (Bombay, Baroda & Central Indian railway), in our area. Their names were displayed boldly on the engines and most cars (compartments). In the mountainous areas of Shimla and Darjeeling and in Gwalior State, there were narrow gauges. There was a published book of schedules (timetable) that most frequent travelers owned.

There were four kinds of trains. 'Mail' trains were named so because they also carried the mail, traveled the main routes connecting major stations, and they also traveled the fastest (I am not sure of the speed), stopped for less than five minutes at major stations and had priority and right of way over other trains on their routes. 'Express' trains traveled at a slightly lower speed and stopped at a few more stations. Occasionally there would be a compartment just for women. 'Passenger' trains stopped at every station and were slower than the express. 'Goods' trains were the slowest and longest, with some open cars, and only carried goods.

There was a deep bend on the approach of the on-coming train, but we could hear its sound and occasionally its whistle as it steamed in. All trains had steam engines fired up with coal. The entire platform seemed to come alive as a train came in, its brakes squealed, and the engine hissed to a stop. People started boarding pell-mell. Coolies boarding and dislodging the luggage onto the racks or under the seats at the direction of the clients. People trying to occupy as much space as they could and become comfortable. Hawkers trying a last-ditch effort to sell their wares. The long engine had a short oblong bump behind the chimney. The coal car was behind it, and the rest of the train was hooked to them. The last compartment was very small and hosted the train's 'Guard'. The guard blew two short-spaced whistles, followed by a long shrill one and waved a green flag, at which the loud train whistle blew, and the train was on its way with several hisses of steam. It all seemed so magical.

Once we got comfortably situated, I would tell my mother that I was hungry. Somehow I got ravenously hungry as soon as our journey began. Mother would take out the puris and make me a wrap with the potatoes and a side of pickle, and I would wolf it down. Once the train went past the urban region, there were vast continuous stretches of agricultural fields on both sides of the train, dotted with small ponds, lakes, and clumps of thatched mud houses with cows grazing or resting, bullocks plowing, and wandering sheep and goats. There were groves of mango and other fruit trees and other signs of an extremely fertile plain. It was a vastly different scenery, soothing and enjoyable.

The train traveled at about 15-20 M.P.H. with a rhythmic sound of the wheels and, if your bogey was upfront, the added sound of the engine. Being a 'passenger' train, it stopped at every station, and more people would board, and a few would get off. Usually, the stop was for 3-4 minutes, except in bigger towns. If you sat at the window and stuck your head out, you could feel the rush of the breeze on your face, and a few particles of coal dust hit it. Sometimes a few would get into your eye. You could never get bored. Most stations were small but bustling with activity. Hawkers selling wares describing their wonders, people coming in and going out of the compartments, people drinking water at a public faucet through a cupped hand (chullu), filling a container, or in animated conversations in the compartment or on the platform. Malnourished, unkempt women and children, dressed in rags, begging for food or coins in pitiable voices were ubiquitous. At certain stops, a man in a blue uniform and a hat would come in. He was the T.T. (ticket checker). He would check and punch your ticket. The ticket was 2"x1" yellowish cardboard, which had the name of the station of purchase, date of purchase, destination, class of travel, and the name of the railway.

It seemed that there were more passengers than seats. There seemed to be an unorganized and silent agreement on the part of the occupants to keep any newcomers out. This was done in interesting ways. People about to board were told that there was no room and to try the next bogey as it had more room. Illiterate ones (the majority of the peasants) were told that it was an 'Intermediate' class and other such fiction. But the arrivals were also wise to these and crowded in anyhow. At first, the seated people would spread out a little to prevent any of the intruders from sitting. Gradually, someone would relent, find and give a little room with a saying, almost unique for the situation and hard to translate adequately.: "You just need a little space in your heart to offer a seat.". Once the intruder got seated, he became part of the earlier occupants, including in trying to prevent the next batch of newcomers from coming in.

On this particular route, very few stations were electrified. After sundown, you could see a faint light or two in the distance till the next station arrived. The traffic was markedly less after sundown, and most stations were lit by only a few kerosene lamp posts casting a dim light. I would doze off with the loss of view outside and the rhythmic sound of the train's wheels. About an hour or so before midnight, depending on how late the train was, and the trains were seldom on time, we arrived at Farrukhabad junction - the end of the line. A junction was a station where trains arrived from many directions to enable passengers to make a connection to their destination on another route. It also had several 'sidings' for the compartments to be detached and reattached to a different train, 'watering' of the engine, and a shed for servicing. Our stop was not much different than the other stations except for being bigger and having a tin shed over the platform. It was not electrified. The coolies came for the luggage, and we climbed down and followed them to the other side of the platform, at the edge of the tin shed. The hold-alls were unrolled, and we lay down on them to sleep. My mother stayed awake, for it was not safe to leave the luggage unguarded, as theft was common. If food was taken out for my parents, stray dogs would hang around for scraps.

Our connecting train to Kannauj would arrive at about 4 a.m. The coolies came back a little before the arrival time and woke us up. Hold-alls were bundled, and we would get ready to board as the train steamed in. It would still be dark, and we would doze off after boarding and awake with the sun coming up on the horizon, ready for breakfast. Mother would dole out the puris and snacks from the bundle. The train ran parallel and alongside a road to its left, a branch of the Grand Trunk road connecting Delhi in the west to Calcutta to the east. Telegraph wires and poles ran between the train and the road. Amazingly, this train originated in Agra! I never did find out why we did not take it as opposed to the route we took. Beyond the road, and on both sides, were farms and mango orchards interrupted by small clusters of houses- the villages. The passing scenery, the cool breeze, and the anticipation of seeing my cousins soon kept me busy. The train stopped at every station. After a few trips, I memorized their names. We would arrive at Kannauj at about 9am. The coolies would come and haul the luggage, and we would disembark and follow the crowd. There were loud voices, "Guttay Kannauj" of hawkers selling thick round cakes of white spun sugar, studded with a few pistachio nuts- called 'Gutta,' from the baskets on their heads, going up and down by the side of the train. The exit was a small gate manned by a T.T. who would take and inspect the ticket. We would head to the ekka stand outside.

My uncle's ekka would be waiting at the stand, and the driver would come up to greet and escort us to it. An ekka is a two-wheeled horse carriage, narrow, with a high canopy supported by four posts and two high-mounted boards on the sides, just above the wooden steel-rimmed wheels. Not very comfortable to sit in, but lighter than a tonga. The difference from other horse carriages made it unique. It was strictly a rural vehicle. The luggage was tied in the back, and two passengers sat in the middle while the other two sat above the wheels. The horse collar had copper bells attached, so its approach could be heard both by the clippity-clop of its hoofs and the jingling of the bells.

The Kannauj train station was in a small hamlet known as Sarai Miran (Miran's Inn), which grew around an old inn, long gone, on the main highway, and now consisted of a few houses, convenience shops, pan and tea shops, and the town courts (tehsil). Across the road was a general mill with a tall chimney and farm fields. It was about two miles from Kannauj. The road to town was a narrow paved road surrounded by fields. Halfway down was a small hut on the dirt by the side of the road with a barrier pole which was always in the raised position. This was the municipal toll booth. An ununiformed man there would signal the traffic to stop, eyeball the contents and then demand a toll or let pass. The toll was on manufactured goods. I don't remember our ekka ever being stopped. Further down on the left were two large playing fields and several brick buildings. This was the hostel for the boys of the local high school.

At the entrance to the town, the paved road ended, and there was an arched gate welcoming the entrants to Kannauj and an ad for a local perfumery that had erected it. The road narrowed considerably and wound around the post office, police station, many closely built multistoried buildings, the entrance to the high school, some perfumeries, then finally to my uncle's place. There was a sharp wide incline leading up to the house with a large open quadrangle on the right, about halfway up. On the left, a few steps lead to a large brick platform and a house. In front of our house was an unpaved open space and then two long steps leading to a verandah on the left and two large thick black wooden doors on the right. The doors were at least seven feet high and about a foot thick and were studded with thick iron knobs, which topped small florets, and a thick high wooden threshold. This was the main entrance to the house.

The doors opened into a small entryway with an in-the-wall cupboard, a door to a long room on the left front of the house, and a narrow doorway with a step up to the right. The right wall had a door that led to a closed staircase to the back. The back of the massive entryway doors had a thick round wooden post across them, which could be slid in and out of place into the brick wall. This entryway was called the 'barotha.' On the other side of the doorway, a step lower, on the right, was a door to the stairs leading up to the room above the barotha and a partially covered roof. This was called 'duchatta.' There was a short wall straight ahead and the entrance to an open paved courtyard to the left and behind the wall. Right behind this short wall were a well and a small raised platform. The courtyard was enclosed by two high walls on the sides. On the left front of the courtyard was a metal grill-covered drain and a raised platform with two niches at its base. The platform had several shallow circular depressions on which sat round baked clay containers with potable water in them - 'ghara's. The back of the courtyard was a verandah with three arches separated by thick ornate pillars. At the other end of the left wall was a door leading to my Uncle's clinic, which was called the 'hospital'. Three ornate doors with semicircular arches above them enclosing stained glass in a fan-shaped pattern, led to a large hall. Its ceiling was at least 16' high. On its back wall, near the ceiling, opened two small balconies. The wall had three in-the- wall cupboards. On the right was a door with a stairway leading to the room (sanchi) with the balconies. At the end of the left wall was a passage leading to the back. At the beginning of the wall was a door leading one step down to another small courtyard (chota aangan). Next to it on the front wall was a small built-in fireplace. All the walls had small arched niches (ala). From the ceiling hung a large crystal chandelier on the right and a large wooden board hung transversely in the center. The right wall had a cupboard in it, and the right front wall had a small opening with a lockable door in it. Behind the hall was a long narrow room with a few steps leading to a small cellar on the right and an opening with metal bars in its back wall. It was always dark there, and it was used as a pantry. The passageway was connected to this room and opened in the back into a tin shed two steps down. To the right, the shed led to a small kitchen and an attached small pantry. In front of the shed was a small paved courtyard with a raised cemented platform all along a high thick wall. To the left of the courtyard was a well with a pulley system above it and a door at the left front corner. The left side was enclosed by the neighbor's high wall and a parapet. The corner door led to a wide verandah with an open courtyard in front of it and facing another verandah and a small room to its left. The left side of that courtyard had a room and an open-fronted covered space. After the verandah was a toilet. The right wall shared the opening for the well. Then there were open steps leading up to the common roof of these buildings. Beyond the toilet was a door opening into a steep, narrow, unpaved lane. This area was rented to a middle-aged couple who had no children. We called them 'Chachcha' (uncle) and 'Chachchi' (auntie), for they were like family.

Coming back to the front of the house, the front verandah led, one step up, to a large room and a small gallery on the left, opening into it by three wide doors. Both sides of this room had in-the-wall, deep cupboards with glass doors and shelves holding medicine bottles and packages. There was a high cornice in the middle of the back wall, a small fireplace, and my uncle's large desk and chair. His medical diploma hung on the wall above the cornice. A door on each side led to the back, which was an open-air courtyard on the left and a tin-covered area on the right. This had a large in-the-wall cupboard with my uncle's surgical instruments and a wide wooden exam table with one end tapering as two boards with a circular space in between, designed by my uncle. The back wall of the room had a platform with a large metal water tank, with a faucet and a concrete sink. Along the left wall of the open space were tiered cement shelves with potted plants on them. The gallery on the left opened in this area. There was a grated open drain there. To the back, there was a narrower room with two wide doors, and many built-in cupboards with multicolored medicine bottles containing liquids, powders, and pills. There was a dispensing counter on the right and a large wooden cupboard on the left. This is where the compounder prepared the medicine from the prescription given to the patient after being seen by my uncle.

From the left of the front verandah, a small upward incline led to another set of buildings. To the right of the incline was a raised unpaved space leading to a high wall, behind which was the Municipal corporation. The buildings consisted of a small front verandah with rooms on each side and an entryway to a large courtyard enclosed by verandahs and some rooms, a well, and a staircase leading to the roof. The front verandah and the room to the right were used as a stable for my uncle's ekka and horse. The rest was rented. The left front was an office and a storage area. This part of the property was called 'Biriya talay,' literally, 'underneath the plum tree.' There was, possibly, a plum tree there at some time.

To the right of the main entrance of the house was a wall beneath which was a platform, then a Neem tree surrounded by a raised cemented area. After that, a few steps descended to the back of the front quadrangle (chautara). To the left of the first step, an ancient stone frieze of 'Vaman Avatar'

(Boar incarnation of Vishnu), about 3' feet square, rested against the cemented area. The entire left side of the quadrangle was a three-storied red building built on a platform about six feet above the narrow street. This was the Haveli, or the main ancestral mansion. Towards the back, near the wall of the Haveli was an L-shaped, open air, door-less toilet, with the bottom of the 'L' acting as the screen. Behind the neem tree was an ornate brick doorway leading to another set of buildings and a large central open space overgrown with scrub bushes, among some ruins. There was a well in the center. All this was walled off, with a large gate opening to a street. This extensive area was the ruins of a ginning mill belonging to the old Tandon family.

The Haveli was an imposing three-storied building built of small polished Indian bricks (Kakaiya eent). Built around the 1870s. It was a rectangular box-like structure with a solitary front entrance through a huge thick doorway, similar to the present residence one described earlier. A small dark foyer (barotha) led to a quadrangle open to the sky. Rooms were built around a corridor surrounding it. This was replicated on the other floors. There was a steep, narrow stairway connecting the floors. To the right, on the first floor, was a well with a pulley system. The only light was what filtered down from above the courtyard. It housed tenants.

Ever Since I could remember, we had been coming to Kannauj during the summer holidays and sometimes around Dussehra. I always looked forward to these visits and had a great time playing with my cousins, or 'cousin brothers' in the Indianized version of the relationship. The older Surendra, four months my junior, and Narendra, two years younger than him. We did nearly everything together. After breakfast, we had our large house to explore and play in. Midmorning, we would go to 'Chachcha, and Chachchi's, for Chachchi always had some snacks for us. She was an excellent cook. She used onion and garlic in her cooking which our family did not. Or we would eat potato stuffed puri rolls called 'choga-moga.' Sometimes my aunt would make fresh 'sev' (short, thin noodles made from chick-pea flour).

The room in the front of the house and the 'barotha' were my Baba's (grandfather) domain. We were allowed to play in it and had free access to it. This room was rectangular and had two windows with deep inside ledges and three in-the-wall closets in the back wall. The closets had lockable doors and belonged to Baba, and the smaller one with a glass door belonged to my cousins, who kept their books there. It was also their study room. On the left window ledge was my grandfather's 'pan' paraphernalia. Several cotton and silk drawstring purses with supari (betel-nut), sliced or whole, the sarota (slicer), pan (betel leaves) wrapped in damp cloth and stored in a hand- made, slide-to-open, wicker container. Round brass containers for choona (calcium paste), katha (catechu), and finely shredded tobacco. From the high ceiling hung a wide wooden board, to which was attached a pleated canvas, about two feet wide. The board had a string that passed over a pulley through a small opening above the entrance to the room. This, like the one in the great hall, was the ceiling fan worked by manpower. (A servant rhythmically pulled the string). High up, above each closet, hung two large pictures of British military officers in uniform with mutton chop sideburns. In between was a large pendulum clock with Roman numerals. On the left wall was a picture of a somewhat scantily clad, plump, blonde, European woman reclined in a seductive pose. Lower down were two small paintings on glass. A horseman and a mysterious figure. The floor was covered with a white sheet over a thin carpet (duree). Against the back wall were two large round pillows (masnad). The front door of the room opened to a paved area. This had two charpais (cots). Grandpa sat on one of these after breakfast, read the newspaper, and interacted with visitors and friends, who used the charpais (cots) to sit on. To the left of the main entrance, on a long platform, were a couple of tall tin drums and a Lota (a small round, half gallon size brass container).

This was grandpa's bath area. His toilet was the one mentioned earlier. He slept on one of the charpais practically all year round after a thin duree (a thin cotton carpet) and sheet were spread on it at night, except in the winter, when the charpais were brought in the room. During the rainy season, the cots were pulled under the verandah in front of my uncle's office.

We would play board games like Ludo and Snakes and Ladders, and Carrom board, or read children's books. Sometimes children from the neighborhood would come over to play. We were not allowed to visit their homes per strict orders of Baba. We also communed with Panditji (real name Dularay Lal), as uncle's compounder was called, when he was not busy. He was a slightly balding man with a small hawkish face and a mustache. He had one good eye, I think the right one, and the other sunken and blind, and a raspy voice. He had to bring up whatever he read close to the good eye. He was from a local Brahmin family, whom my uncle had trained since he was a youth to compound and dispense medicines, give injections and dress minor wounds. His designation was 'Compounder,' and all patients called him 'compounder saheb' as a mark of respect. He smoked biris (tobacco wrapped in a cone shaped dried leaf), and when we got older, told us bawdy jokes or couplets.

Lunch was around 1 p.m. Baba was the first to come in and eat. My uncle would wind up the morning session with Panditji sitting across the table from him with the day's prescriptions and give him the breakdown of the collection per prescription, and hand over the few rupee notes (paper currency) and a lot of change. My uncle would enter the house from the side door, and Panditji would lock up. Uncle would then unlock his cupboard and enter the morning's take in a notebook and arrange it in neat piles of notes (bills) and change, stacked according to their denominations. The middle shelf had money, and the upper and lower shelves had his clothes and other belongings. The keys to the cupboard and the medicine cupboards hung from the end of his janaiu. In the summer, he would bathe again from a bucket in the tidwari (verandah) of the great hall. All the while, he would be conversing with someone. He was jovial and inquisitive, especially if the morning's collection was good or exceeded his expectations. If not, there was a good chance he would chastise us for being careless and find fault with things. We learned to sense his moods and be around when he was in a good mood or scatter when he was not. Most of the time, he was in a good mood.

Large parcels of medications would arrive. We were recruited to open them and help place them in the cupboards in my uncle's office. I loved to do that. I learned the names of some medicines and pharmaceutical companies. Ciba, Park-Davis, May & Baker, Pfizer, and Bayer. I don't remember the names of any medicines, but the letters B.P. and U.S.P. after their names fascinated me. I recalled these letters in my third year of medical college and finally understood them (British and United States Pharmacopeia) and smiled at the nostalgia from my boyhood!

Till I was seven years old, these trips involved going to summer school in the morning. We had our Patti (a rectangular, polished, black wooden board with a small diamond-shaped head at the top), a budakka (two small bowls of baked clay joined by a carrying handle and containing kharia (white chalk paste), and a kalam (pen made of reed), which we carried to the school. This was a room in the large house down the lane behind Chachchi's. Three or four boys from the house joined us. An old Pandit (Brahmin) was our teacher. I learned the Hindi alphabet here. We also did basic arithmetic and learnt times tables in Hindi. Panditji had a cane and did not hesitate to use it on our heads when he saw fit.

My cousins and I did nearly everything together. We used the small platform to the left of the house as our toilet, which was a pair of bricks for each of us to squat on. Water was used by everyone for post-toilet cleansing. Hands were washed with clean clay or sand used as a detergent. We wore home-made shorts with drawstrings, sleeveless tops and roamed around barefoot, and used chappals (Indian slippers) when we had to go somewhere. Winter wear was naiker (shorts) and shirt, home-knitted hand -me -down woolen sweaters and woolen Chester (coats) of Ravi Bhaiya, Sidya and Vidya Bahen. The times I visited during Dussehra holidays, we went with Kunji,(the servant) to see the Ram Lila (enactment of Lord Rama's life) at the nearby Golmaidan (name of the commons), where we had cotton candy, and peanuts and bought toys.

Sometimes we went on picnics at local temples, Gaurishankaran and Chintaman, locally. To Tirwa, about five miles away, and to Akin ghat, about ten miles away, which was on the banks of the Ganga. Uncle had donated its main idol, a Shivalinga (Shiva idol) found in our haveli. We went by uncle's ekka and later on the tonga, so it was an all-day trip. Bathing in the Ganga was considered holy. We always went with Kunji, the house servant. The Ganga at Kannauj was about a mile away, and my mom, aunt, and Chachchi would walk there, early in the morning, on certain holy days. The distance varied, for the meandering Ganga changed its course frequently.

We played in our chautara (the large courtyard in the front), for Baba would not let us go anywhere else to play. Despite caste differences, we played without any discrimination with whoever was available. I remember playing with a kahar (a lower caste) boy named Tillu, who was very good at most of our games. All the games were simple and inexpensive. The most expensive item was a rubber ball! We played a game called Dhoosi-baila, with two teams. Five or seven small flat stones would be stacked, then from a line drawn in the dirt, a few feet away, a member of one team would try to knock down the stack with the ball, as the other team stood on the other side. The player had three tries. If he failed to knock down the stack or if the ball was caught by the other side without a bounce, the striker was 'out.' If it was struck, the striking team had to restack it, and the other team tried to hit as many players on the striking team with the ball. If three players were hit before they could restack, that team was 'out.' But if you restacked it before that, you got another chance.

Gilli- danda was a two-team sport. We made a gilli out of a four-inch piece of round wood, sharpening the ends to a point. Danda was a round stick, an inch thick and about two feet long. A shallow, three-inch-long vertical area was dug in the dirt, and the gilli was placed across it. A member of one team heaved the gilli with the danda as far as he could while the opposing team stood in front. If the gilli was caught, the hurler was out. If the gilli landed uncaught, the opposing team tried to hit the danda placed across the launching groove. If it was hit, the launching team was out. If not, the launcher went to it and struck one end with the danda and, as it whirled up, hit it as hard as he could. If it was caught, the striker was out. If he missed, the sticker had two other chances. The other team picked up the gilli, where it landed on the last try, and tried to hit the danda, which was placed across the launch pit. If the danda was hit, the side was out. If not, the distance where it had landed would be measured with the danda, and that would be the launching team's score. You had to be careful so as not to get hit by the gilli, for it could hurt! There were stories of kids losing an eye, but we never saw that, and none of us could hit that hard and tried to stay away from the line of fire.

Kabaddi was another great game. There were four or five kids on each team separated by a line in a fair-sized square area. One player crosses over to the opposing team's side, continuously repeating the word 'Kabaddi' in just one breath and tags as many players as possible, and returns. The other team tried to catch and hold him on their side. The number of players touched and a successful return still saying 'kabaddi' in the same breath were 'out.' If the player got caught and could not get back or stopped saying kabaddi, he was out.

Kite flying was very common in Kannauj, mostly in the summer, from late afternoon to sundown. The kites were square-shaped with a thin bamboo frame, with one point of the square as the top and a semi-circular strip of bamboo joining the two sides and one vertical one joining the top and bottom. The bottom had a small square patch, slightly jutting out and holding the bottom of the frame together. They came in several sizes, but the usual size was about 18" on each side. Sticking a thin paper tail to the bottom was optional. One end of a string was tied to the vertical mid-piece of the frame near the arched part, another to it near the bottom, and tied together about a foot from the kite. To this was tied the first part of the long thin string called the 'manja,' which was about a hundred feet long. This was thin but extremely sharp. Sometimes it was coated with powdered glass. The rest of the string was called 'saddi' and was slightly thicker and not as sharp. All of the string was wound around a 'charkhi' (shaped like a rolling pin). The manja was the business end in a kite-fight. Kites were flown from the flat roofs of houses by children or teenagers, though some adults also did so. The sky would be dotted with kites of various sizes and colors at different heights. Tares in the kites were repaired with patches using boiled potato as glue, for kites were relatively expensive for teenagers.

The enjoyment of kite flying was enhanced by kite fights (paich). The idea was to attack another kite and cut its string. There were many strategies. Attacking from above and pulling your kite sharply. Or from below or encircling it. This was done by the sharp manja portion of the string. You had to be careful not to cut your finger/fingers on the manja. There were favorite colors and colorful sayings about kites. 'Hari haravai, lal jitavai, kali kat kat lai avai' (green defeats, red wins, and black cuts), was one. The exhilaration of cutting an opponent's kite, or two if lucky, in an evening was indescribable. It was frequent to see a kid or kids chasing after a kite as it slowly descended after being cut, to capture it. Some adults took part in competitions where bets were made, or a five or ten rupee note would be affixed to the kite as a dare. My cousin Surendra (Baby) loved the sport and was very good at it. I learned and flew a kite sometimes, but I was not crazy about it.

During the early 1950s, Uncle got rid of the ekka and, for some years, had a tonga. Then he bought a used station wagon type of car and employed a chauffeur. I remember one time he came down to Agra with Mahashay baba (Baba's cousin). He bought clay and papier- mache toys to sell at the Ram Lila fairs at Kannauj. On his way back, I went with him. We started in the early morning on the approximately 125-mile journey. The paved road was about 15' wide and, at times, with only about a ribbon of a dirt shoulder and many ruts. It was shared with bullock carts, bicyclists, and small herds of cattle, sheep, goats, and stray dogs. There was an occasional car or bus. I was excited because I had been in a motor vehicle only a few times. There was plenty of dust. After some roadside stops, we reached Mainpuri, a small town, in the late afternoon, where we had lunch, which mom had packed for us, supplemented by dessert from uncle's favorite sweets shop at the stop. We had several more stops for tea, snacks, and gas (petrol), which was only available in bigger towns, passed through many more small towns, and arrived home at Kannauj around 9 p.m. After around 15 hours!

A couple of years later, my uncle got rid of that car, for it died. He bought a green Chevrolet from his old medical school professor in Agra, Dr. Ghulam Murtaza, who was migrating to Pakistan. He had become interested in local politics and ran for the municipal council in alliance with his friend, Khan Saheb. The entire Khatri community and our neighbors were on the other side, which caused some strain on the community. It was summer, and all of us kids were recruited to help. I learned about voting lists, canvassing, and the procedure to challenge a vote, and I met influential local people and learned how to influence them (some by supplying them with alcohol!). I went around town on a tonga, with a portable loudspeaker announcing our party's candidates and soliciting votes. Uncle and his friend won. I got a hands-on education about grassroots politics and elections.

Grandpa (Baba)

Grandpa was about five feet four inches, slightly overweight, with a prominent belly, brown complexion, a prominent white walrus mustache, bald, handsome features, a prominent scar on the forehead, and an authoritarian demeanor. He wore a white dhoti (a wrap-around cotton lower garment), under which was a sizable belly and a bulge of a huge hernia. His white hairy chest was bare except in winter when he wore a Bandi (quilted Indian jacket) and Kantopa (quilted cap with broad chin straps). Over the left shoulder, across the chest, hung the three-stringed Janaiu (sacred thread) from the right end of which, just below the hip, hung his key chain. Sometimes he would put on a Kurta (a collarless Indian shirt). At home, he was mostly barefoot. He would wear kharaon (wooden platforms with a knob between the first and second toes) to the toilet. He was a man of fixed routine. In the morning, after the toilet, he would brush his teeth with a neem datun (a six inch twig of the neem tree with the business end made fibrous by crushing it). He was served his breakfast outside. He would then do any supervising needed, such as, cleaning of Uncle's office, the front courtyards and the care and feeding of the horse, and other such matters. His friends and contemporaries would arrive, and they would shoot the breeze. People would come and go all morning long. He would also find time to read the Hindi newspaper.

Across the street was a small Shivala (Shiva temple) on a high paved platform. A few steps below it was the neighborhood's 'sweet' (potable) water well. It had pulleys suspended from an iron framework on four sides and bustled with activity from early morning to late night, being the only source of potable water for the neighborhood. Some people also bathed on the ample platform around the well. Below that, at the street level, was a stone trough, filled by the water spilled around the well, for the passing horses of ekkas and stray cows and bulls. Several men from the area bathed at the well in the late morning and occasionally carried out conversation or just greetings with grandpa. One such person I remember was Budhoo baba, a very handsome man, white-skinned, with a booming voice. He joked with the young women who fetched water from the well, and they poured water over him, for I never saw him draw water. He came with an Angocha (a thin Indian towel with red print) and some soap. He would also joke with grandpa across the street, for they were contemporaries. In summer time the municipal corporation would 'disinfect' the wells by putting potassium permanganate in them. It would make the water pinkish for a few days.

Around noon time, Grandpa bathed with water from the drums on the platform outside, using the Lota to pour it over his body and change into another dhoti. He would then wait for the ekka traffic to increase. This was the signal that the train from Kanpur had arrived, also signaling lunchtime. He would then proceed, bare-chested, except in the winter, to the kitchen area, a Lota full of potable water in his right hand and the keys attached to his janaiu (sacred thread) jangling against the Lota and signaling his arrival for lunch. He sat on a patra (a small, low, wooden platform) and was served on a thali (round metal tray) and small round metal containers with dal and vegetable curry in them. Sometimes my mother or aunt would fan him with a hand held fan. He would make a bland remark or two and, when finished, rinse his mouth and depart to his room. Occasionally he would make a snide remark as he passed grandma, seated on a charpai (cot), in the great room, just to get a rise out of her. They were not on speaking terms. She would mostly ignore it, or fume with a response addressed to whoever was nearby, never to him directly. Both my mother and my aunt covered their head and part of the upper face with the top of the dhotis. It was the custom to do that in the presence of elders. Married women always had their heads covered. Grandpa would then prepare a pan in his room, chew on it as he pulled out the small Ramayan (a holy book about the life of Lord Rama), lay down on the carpeted floor, and read it before taking his afternoon nap. In the summer, a servant boy would pull rhythmically on the rope attached to the ceiling fan to fan him from the barotha.

We called grandpa Baba, which is what a father's father is called in Hindi. His official name was Shiv Charan Lal, but everyone called him Channu babu. I don't know why. When we were little, we would rub his chest, scratch his back, massage his legs and feet, and play with his janaiu, but this stopped as we grew older. He led a simple regulated life. He used the toilet before breakfast, lunch, and dinner. He would light up a cigarette, wind the right side of the janaiu around his right ear as he walked to the toilet with a Lota full of water for ablution and smoke in there. The winding of the janaiu was done to avoid it being desecrated by it touching the ground while defecating or urinating. He only smoked these three times. He smoked a brand called Passing Show. The pack of ten had a picture of an English gentleman in a top hat, a monocle, and a cane under his arm.

Baba was multi-talented. He knew a lot about a lot of things. When there would be a wedding in the local Khatri community, he would be requested to supervise the cooking of the food by halwais (hired cooks). This included keeping an eye out for theft, wastage, and quality. Since nearly all clothes were tailored by the family tailor, he would oversee the amount of cloth required and, at times, show the tailor how to utilize the material with maximum efficiency and also prevent theft, as the tailor tried to ask for extra cloth to save some for himself, or so it was thought. Our family had a tailor (darzi), barber (nai), clothes washer-woman, (dhoban) potter (kumbhar), mason (mistry), midwife (dai) , sweeper and night-soil remover (bhangi), oilman (taily), local priest (padha), family priest (purohit), a dish-washer woman (kaharan). Some of them had their families serving ours for a few generations. We shared these workers with other families. All these were treated with respect by the youngsters in the family, and sometimes appellations of an uncle, brother, sister, sister–in–law, and grandpa (baba) were suffixed to their name. Most liked and accepted this but still remained cognizant of their station in life. Of these, only the bhangi were the untouchables.

The Indian collarless shirt, the 'kurta,' open at the chest, was commonly made of muslin. It was the fashion to wear it starched, with the long sleeves corrugated, giving them a pleasing appearance. This could only be done if the sleeve was stiff, hence the starching, and was done by means of a large, polished, hollowed cowrie shell. The cowrie shell was placed at the end of the sleeve and was then dragged up toward the shoulder, creating corrugations all along. This was not as easy to do as it sounds. But Baba was a master at it. We tried to learn the craft, but only my younger cousin (Narendra) Kallu could do it reasonably well. Baba could also cook. He would occasionally cook goat meat sent by one of my uncle's Muslim patients. This was done with great fanfare on a separate open-top Indian oven (chulha), under the tin shed near the kitchen, much to the disgust of the female folk in the family. Baba would select the spices and have the servant grind them to the desired consistency, sauté onions, and prepare the goat meat in one of the many recipes he had, all in his head. We ate it separately from the rest of the family in glass and china dishes; for the family metal utensils could not be contaminated with meat. The dish would be shared with a neighboring Muslim family and the male (Chachcha) of the couple renting the portion at the back of the house. Only Baba and we male cousins ate the dish; my uncle ate very rarely, and my dad never. He was an excellent cook, and I learned the name of some of the dishes, e.g., Roganjosh, Kharey masalay ka gosht, Keema, Do-pyada, and that the gravy was called "shurua' (shorva) in the dialect. I think I enjoyed more of the rebellious, forbidden nature of it and the company more than the dish itself.

Baba had many likes and dislikes. He liked the company and the people listening to his stories. He did not like men without any facial hair on the upper lip. Once, cousin Surendra (Baby) shaved his upper lip, and Baba admonished him, saying it looked like his behind. Baby was his favorite grandson. He was also a little stricter with him. Baby was the recipient of a mild strike or two on his head when Baba thought he was cheeky or disobedient. When we were children, he would not allow us to go play at our friends' places, saying that if they wanted to play, they could come to our place. He disliked the shake of a head as an answer for "yes' or no.' He would say, "Why don't you move your tongue, which weighs an ounce, instead of your head which weighs a ton!" When offered only a small amount of a dish he liked, he would bend his neck, point to his ear, and sarcastically say, "Pour it in my ear!"

He had no source of income. Father and uncle gave him an allowance every month to cover his expenses. These were mainly his pan and tobacco and the evening desert he would get for himself from the bazaar. Apparently, the money from my father was either sporadic or delayed. He never asked for it directly, but when father visited, Baba would take his sewing kit out and start mending an old dhoti (lower garment) to indicate the extent of his poverty and shame him into buying a new one or paying up any arrears. He would also say to us that your father has not kept up his promise. I think I was nine or ten years old at the time, and the allowance was two rupees a month. He would tell us not to get too attached to money as it was the root cause of all evil. Father with son, brother with brother, friend with friend, all fight over money. It was easy for him to say, for he never had any, but maybe he was saying it based on what he saw in the past in his own family. However, it was great advice, and I tucked it away in my memory for future use.

Grandma was called Baua by everyone. Nobody had any idea why. If she knew, she did not tell us, and nobody seemed to be inquisitive enough to ask. Her real name, I found out later, was Phoolmati Devi. She was an imposing woman with a long face, thin lips, a broad nose, large gray-green eyes, and white skin and thin hair. She seldom smiled, spoke little, and her words seemed to carry weight in the family. Both her daughters-in-law, (my mother and aunt), were extremely deferential towards her, as was most everyone else. She never asked for anything directly. It was always in an indirect manner or a suggestion, e.g., "Maybe I might have another roti." She liked her paratha crisp, and I remember my mom pressing it on the tava (hot plate) with a batta (flat mortar stone) to make it crisp. She had the first of the three deep-in –the wall cupboards in the great room. On its shelves were all her possessions. She also supervised the servant and the evening cook. She sat on a square, low stool (chowki) or a small bare charpai near the door to the small courtyard (chota angan). Her main job was to oversee the ordering and procurement of the daily vegetables. Uncle's compounder, after finishing his job at the dispensary, would be given a rupee note. He would stop at Baua's, get the order, go through the backdoor and Chachchi's house to the vegetable market in town, not far, and come back with the order in the cloth bags he took with him. He then gave an accounting of the amount and price of the purchase, as it was spread out, to Baua, and returned the change, if any, to her. She would take stock, comment on the product, and have the servant take it to the kitchen. The change was hers to keep. She was very affectionate with us.

She would fan us with her hand fan, make sure we ate and give us treats from her cupboard. At night we would lie down beside her, and she would tell us stories and common folk puzzles or sing ditties. She was partial to Ravi Bhaiya. She would make sure he was taken care of in every way without expressing her love overtly. I think it was because his mother died when he was young. She didn't have to, as I think he was treated better than any of us, being the oldest male child in the family. Occasionally she would get angry about something and would go up to the roof above the front of the house (duchatta) and sit under the tin shed, against the long window, with bars, overlooking the inner part of the house. When my grandfather would see that, he would snidely remark that she was in her "sulking house" (cope-bhavan, in Hindi). Her meals were sent up to her, and I am sure she was coaxed and cajoled to come down, for she was never there for more than a few hours. I never did learn what brought about these rare occurrences. I loved her.

Uncle (Chacha)

My uncle was of medium height, very fair skinned, with wavy hair, a prominent but pleasant nose- an easy smile and demeanor. Unlike my father, he interacted with everyone in the family easily and pleasantly and was talkative. His name was Kailash Nath, but his 'pet' name was Dullu, though I did not hear anyone call him that. He would go to his clinic, which we called 'hospital,' through the side door in the main courtyard right after an early breakfast. Before leaving, he would prepare himself a pan and touch a large picture of Lord Shiva and then his forehead. On the left side of the verandah before the great room was a wide shelf with the picture of Lord Shiva on the right, followed by a large mirror and below it, all the ingredients of preparing a pan. On the opposite side was a niche for many idols and a takhat (a wooden platform) – where grandma, my aunt, and mom did their puja (worship). He wore pants and a jacket in the winter and a dhoti (lower wrap-around garment) and kameez (shirt) in the warmer weather. He bundled up in cold weather when he was in the house because he was more sensitive to it.

Dulary Lal

He was my uncle's compounder mentioned earlier. Everyone called him Pandit or Pandit ji. The job of a compounder was to prepare and dispense the prescriptions written by my uncle. There were very few patent medicines, so the doctors wrote the ingredients and their amounts as a prescription (liquid mixture, powder, or ointment) and instructions of usage, which were then prepared and dispensed in glass bottles, old newspapers, or small round wooden containers. Uncle wrote the charge amount in one corner of the prescription, and Pandit ji collected that from the patient. There was no separate consulting fee. When my uncle went for a house call, Pandit ji would read the newspaper next to Baba, kibitz with a visitor or tell us bawdy couplets, limericks, or jokes. He smoked biris (tobacco wrapped in a short cone-shaped dried leaf). He had basic education and had been trained by my uncle and worked with him since he was a teenager.

Chachi

Chachi (father's younger brother's wife) was called that by all of us as we grew up hearing her addressed as such by Vidya Bahen (the oldest child in the family). Baua and Baba called her Kanpurwali (one from Kanpur). She was tall, light skinned, jovial, loving, practical, and an extrovert. She enjoyed seeing a passing procession, music, radio, and cinema (when in Agra) and was a good cook. She loved, respected, and got along well with my mother. She was not a stickler for old rules and would adjust and bend according to the situation. Without question, Baby, her older son was the apple of her eye, though she treated all of us well. I loved my aunt.

Chachcha and Chachchi

These are variants of the word chacha (father's younger brother) and chachi (Chacha's wife). We called the tenants living at the back of our house by those names, probably to avoid confusion with chacha (my uncle) and chachi. Chachcha was a dark, middle-aged man, from the trading caste, who was in the wholesale business of selling gur (jaggery). He was quiet, affectionate, and liked to eat rich food. For a while, he kept a water buffalo in his courtyard. Chachchi was dark and nice looking, very affectionate, an excellent cook, and spent quite a bit of her time at our place.

They were childless and treated us as their own children. They also had a parrot in a cage. Gradually, they, especially Chachchi, became part of the family. Their rent was four annas, (about 3 cents in current value) per month. Chacchcha died suddenly in his late fifties. Uncle stopped charging chachchi any rent thereafter.

Kunji

Kunji was the house servant. He was wiry, middle-aged, had a jovial face, close-cropped hair with a choti (tuft of hair at the crown). He came early in the morning, stacked away the charpais, rolled the beddings, put away the lanterns, and broomed the floors with a jharoo (about a three foot broom made of long plant fibers). He then fetched potable water from the well across from the house and filled up all the gharas, and the drums from the well in the house, which was brackish and used for washing, and other household needs. I remember going with him to get freshly puffed laiya (rice) and chana (chickpeas) from the baker's oven. It smelled so good! And it was our favorite snack. He went home after lunch, around two o'clock, and returned around four. He replenished the water, went to the bazaar to fetch things, collected all the lanterns, checked their kerosene, lit and placed them back at their needed places, replenished the diyas (oil lamps) in the alas (niches) with mustard oil, and lit them. He was great with us, except that he would scold us when we wasted potable water, for fetching it was hard work. His one talent was unique. He could fart loudly on demand! We thought it was so cool and asked him frequently to do that, and if he had time, he would oblige. I liked him very much. And I was really sad, when many years later, in medical college, I learned that he had passed away.

Other workers

The woman who washed the dishes was called Dulhainia (bride or daughter-in-law) by the adults and Bhauji (brother's wife) by us. She was short, dark, good-looking, and good-natured, bedecked in silver jewelry of bangles and ankle rings, had a high-pitched voice, and was in her late twenties or early thirties. We used to tease her and kid with her. She belonged to the Kahar sub-caste. The men from this sub-caste were originally doli (palanquin) carriers, transporting people, mostly women. There was a maharajin who cooked dinner. But I don't remember her too well. Maharajins were Brahmin women, usually widows, who worked to make ends meet. It had to be a Brahmin, for no other caste was allowed to be in the kitchen. In our family in Kannauj, the evening meal was always prepared by a maharajin.

The family darzi (tailor) was Sutalli miyan. He was a thin, dark Muslim who would be called in when new clothes were to be made. He came with a steel yardstick, measuring tape, and scissors. The material was shown to him; he would take measurements and ask for the estimated length of the material. That's where Baba came in. He would tell him ways to save material and utilize it well. Sometimes they argued a bit. The idea was to maximize utilization. Also, tailors were suspected of taking more material than needed. The family mistry (mason) was Bali miyan (local pronunciation of the Arabic Wali). He was a tall thin Muslim man. There was a nai (barber), an older man who came twice a week to shave Baba, using an old-fashioned razor, which he sharpened on a small leather strap, and also trimmed his nails and hair. He also gave a haircut to my uncle and cousins. He belonged to the Nai sub-caste. They were also used as messengers and go-betweens in marriages. The Nai women massaged female members of the family as needed, especially women after childbirth. Dhobi (washer man) was another sub caste. They usually did the washing on the banks of a river. The clothes were boiled in large caldrons or beaten against a stone slab, washed, and hung on make-shift lines to dry on the banks.

Taily (oilman) dealt with oils, mostly it's retailing. Their women folk also did massages for women of higher castes.

Every Saturday, a taily young man would come to the barotha of the house with a copper plate and a metal container with mustard oil in it, and say, "Saneecher devata raksha karain". (May the Saturn god protect you), and was given a coin. Apparently to guard from evil, for Saturday was considered inauspicious. Chamars (leather workers) were shoemakers and repairers, makers of other leather goods and worked with hides. They were often seen at street corners with their trademark iron anvils, repairing and re-soling footwear or repairing other small leather goods. These were called 'mochis' (cobbler). Bhangis were removers of 'night soil', and cleaners of toilets, street drains, and street sweepers. The last two were the only 'untouchable' castes. All castes were hereditary.

There were also some itinerant professionals. To me, the most fascinating was the Dhunna (fluffer). This was a man who was given flattened-down, cotton- stuffed quilts and pillows. He disemboweled them of the flattened cotton and, then, with a large bow-shaped gadget, carded or fluffed up the flattened cotton, as if rejuvenating it! A Lohaar (iron worker) would come to sharpen dull knives and scissors and repair tongs and other household metal gadgets.)

Family friends, and visitors came over, mornings and evenings every day. Some stand out in memory. Mana dada

(dada-older brother) was a childhood friend of my uncle. He was a dark skinned affable man with a prominent nose and belonged to a group of Bhattacharya (Brahmin caste) families who lived in our neighborhood. He had no employment, and I don't think he ever did. He came in the morning and evening. In the mornings, he would mostly converse with Baba, and whoever else was visiting and had pan and tobacco. In the evening, he joined the company of many other friends of my Uncle, who visited nearly every day. There would be bare charpais and a few chairs put out under the neem tree, on which people would make themselves comfortable and converse on personal, local, regional, national and political matters, retell old stories, reminisce, and even doze off. These gatherings usually ended around dinner time, between eight and nine o' clock.

Children were not part of the gathering, but I loved to hear the old tales and sometimes hung around unobserved in the periphery. One of the stories I heard was that many years ago, a family in the neighborhood was very poor but too proud to ask for help. The man of the house kept pigeons and would release them in the daytime. They would feed in the grain fields and fly back to his rooftop. He would feed them warm water, which would make them regurgitate the grain. Several such trips by the pigeons would provide enough grain for the family to eat. Even at that age (7 or 8yrs), I was fascinated by the sheer inventiveness and implausibility of the story. Another story was of my Baba waking up in the middle of the night on the roof of the Haveli, when he was young and seeing a congregation of parees (fairies) on the Bala peer (great Muslim holy man), two large tombs, visible in the distance, on a large hill, about a quarter of a mile away.

Sometimes people would fall asleep and had to be awakened and reminded to go home. Uncle smoked a hookah for a brief period, for he had bouts of kidney stone colic. It was thought to help alleviate that. Mana dada often accompanied my uncle when he went out of town. It did not matter for how long and how far. Of course, my uncle took care of all expenses. Life was unhurried; people had plenty of time, few needs and expenses, and accepted things as they were and their situation in life, at least in small towns like Kannauj.

Pratap chacha lived close by and was a childhood friend of my uncle. He was a good-looking jovial man, belonging to the large Kapoor clan who were in the perfume business. Their factory and shop were across from our driveway. He visited frequently when in town, for he was often away on business. He had free access to our house and would walk right in if uncle was busy and converse with whoever was available. Some of his three brothers also visited. Every time any of them came, a wonderful whiff of perfume accompanied them. Two of his sons, of our age group, were also our playmates. Their shop faced the main street where his dad, Ram Narayan, baba, sat on a cushion with a masnad (large round pillow) at his back. He was stern, and we were scared of him. He also sold official postcards, envelopes, and postage stamps. Since the post office was far away, we were often sent to get these from him. He never visited us.

Mahasay baba was Baba's first cousin, son of his maternal aunt. He was short and had a prominent nose, quiet, and about a dozen years younger. He lived not too far and would come once or twice a day and have breakfast with him. He was my uncle's go-to person for his local business ventures and often his travels.

Haji ji was a short, stocky Muslim man with a pockmarked face and a henna- dyed beard. He was Baba's contemporary, came mid-mornings and mostly conversed with him, sometimes given tea and always paan and tobacco.

Ansari saheb was a dark, middle-aged Muslim who rented the Birya Talay buildings and was the regional agent for the Brooke-Bond tea company. He would join the gathering in the evenings. His wife frequently visited with my aunt.

Khan Saheb was a short, wiry man, from a prominent local landowning (zamindar) Muslim family, and a friend and a political ally of my uncle, ever since my uncle ran for the municipal council. He visited occasionally, always with uncle in the clinic, dressed in a pajama, kurta, and a dupalli topi (a small muslin cap) and carried a silver-topped cane.

Early in the morning, Baba had a special group of visitors his own age. They were Khunni baba, Unoo baba, and Daddu. They would come after their morning walk and sit on the charpais and shoot the breeze for a short while. Khunni baba was a ruddy-faced, well-built man, a Tandon, not related to us, who had his perfumery business on the main road next to the Kapoor's. We could see the top stories of his large house from our place. Unnu baba was thin and tall. There were many tales about him, but the one I remember is that he went to the bathroom every thirty days or so! Daddu was thin and slightly stooped over but active and lived in the house to the left of our driveway. They sometimes used a datoon (twig of the neem tree with one end crushed) on their teeth while visiting and talked mostly of the good old days.

The women had their separate social lives. In late afternoons, a servant would be sent to the home of the women they wanted to visit, to check if it was alright to visit, and if so, they went over, heads /faces covered, wrapped in a chador or shawl, and escorted by the servant. They would take their knitting, crocheting, cantaloupe seeds for cracking-open, with them, to work on as they chatted and got local news and gossip.

Most people from Kannauj were optimistic, liked to joke around, and were friendly. Life was unhurried, wants were few, changes slow, and contentment level high. Time seemed to have slowed down, and that was O.K. with them. Men dressed alike, in shirts or kurtas, and the male dhoti, no matter what their occupation or social or financial status.

We would frequently get 'marori' (heat rash) on our forearms which was treated with sandalwood paste. We would also get boils on the skin, which were treated with the application of neem paste and the larger ones with belladonna plaster patches or Magsulf paste. Frequent gastro-intestinal complaints meant a visit to Panditji, who would give us a dose of a 'carminative mixture' or a pill of sulfa guanidine. Cuts and bruises were treated with the applications of tincture of iodine. The various courtyards and the large house made it a great place to play or just wander around. There were also more people to interact with. I enjoyed my visits to Kannauj and looked forward to them. Though in separate cities, it kept both branches of the family united as one, and my cousins were my brothers and sisters, just living in different places. Baba always reinforced this relationship by admonishing us if he heard any of us say," It is mine," by correcting us and making us say, "It is ours."

Shruti (Lore-or that which is herd)

We belong to the Khatri caste, the 'warrior' caste, second of the four castes of the ancient Aryan system of Brahmin (priests), Kshatriyas (warriors), and Vaishyas (tradesmen) Shudras (workers). The term Kshatriya became 'Khatri' as Sanskrit evolved and changed. All Khatris claim origin in the Punjab where 'Ksh' is pronounced as 'Kh.' At the time of the reign of Allah-ud- din Khilji (13- !4th A.D.), they were part of his army fighting in south India and suffered heavy casualties. This resulted in a huge number of young Khatri widows who became destitute. Since widow marriage was not practiced by Hindus, they demonstrated and wailed outside the emperor's palace in grief and for relief. When he enquired, the problem was explained to him. He forbade the Khatris from the army. Having been banned from the military, they took up other professions- mainly trade, and prospered. Eventually, they spread out, dominating most trades from Afghanistan to Bengal and beyond. They kept up their caste traditions of wearing the janaiu (sacred thread), weapon puja, and others. They rose to high positions under many rulers, e.g., Raja Todar Mal Tandon was a minister in Akbar's Mughal court. All the Sikh Gurus, including Nanak, the founder, were Khatris.

I can trace the family eleven generations, to Vrindavan Tandon, in the early 1700s A.D. The details about his origin have been lost due to the dying out of the family of our hereditary family priest, who had kept the records. We belong to the 'solar' race, descended from sage Angiras (gotra). The 'kuldevi' (family deity) is Chandika. The family priests are of the Saraswat Brahmin caste. In Hindu tradition, only the male side of the genealogy was followed, not because of male chauvinism but because daughters were considered belonging to another family (the family they were going to be married into). When there was a major religious ceremony, like janaiu or marriage, the family priest would recite the names of all known ancestors of the person involved. Our priest made us memorize a few, e.g., Birendra, son of Harihar Nath, son of Shiv Charan Lal, son of Gaurishankar, son of Kanauji Lal, son of Angad Rai, son of Ramcharan – phew! It ended with 'Vermahum'- meaning we are Verma, of which I do not know the significance.

Angad Rai came from across the Ganga from Ganj Moradabad to Kannauj during the U.P. famine of 1837 or around the time of Ghadar (Great Indian Mutiny) of

1857.His son Kanaujilal did extremely well in Indigo farming.

Kanaujilal had five sons. Visheshur Nath, Laxmi Narayan, Gaurishankar, Shiva Shankar, and Madan Lal. Visheshur Nath, the eldest, ran the business, prospered, acquired about fifty-two villages, built the haveli (family mansion), and set up headquarters in Kanpur. Indigo was transported to Calcutta via Kanpur and Patna by boat on the Ganga and then exported. His brothers stayed in Kanpur. The family acquired the trappings of the very rich of the day. Patronizing of 'dance girls', mehfils (gatherings of acolytes and hanger-ons), alcohol, etc. This was relatively short-lived as indigo was synthesized in Germany, and the market for their product dried up. They tried to set up a cotton ginning business at Kannauj, which failed and incurred massive losses. Visheshur Nath refused to declare bankruptcy due to pride and lost everything. This led to quarreling among the brothers, and the family broke up.

Visheshur Nath was a good-looking proud man, who built and expanded the business, and saw its destruction. He rubbed shoulders with the wealthy in Kanpur and Kannauj. Moti Lal Nehru (the father of the first prime minister of India, Jawaharlal Nehru), a leading lawyer in the province, represented him in some litigation at the provincial High

Court at Allahabad. He had no children. The main room of the house, where my uncle lived, was where he held court, and had music and entertainment sessions with dancing girls, whom he patronized. It was also the place for drinking and eating non-vegetarian food for which he had a Kashmiri cook. When the wealth vanished, so did the hanger-ons. In his last days, he lived with his wife in a building behind the Haveli, estranged from his family, and abandoned by friends, a bitter and broken man. His anguish and repentance are manifest in the hundred odd bhajans (religious compositions) he wrote in exquisite handwriting in his later years. My father retrieved them after he died.

Gaurishankar, Baba's father, died of acute arsenic poisoning at the age of 23yrs. Arsenic was used in the burnt form as an aphrodisiac. Apparently, the person preparing it did not do a good job, and despite his brother's frantic efforts and consulting British physicians in Kanpur, he died. He left a girl, and a boy (Baba) born a few months after his death, and a young widow. Baba was brought up by his uncle Visheshur Nath.

Shiv Shankar, Laxmi Narain, and Madan Lal divided up the properties in Kanpur and settled there. They also had shares in the Haveli. I do not know much about them except for Madan Lal, the youngest, who married twice and had two sons by his younger wife, who were much younger than my father and uncle!

I could not find out the year of my grandfather's birth, but by some approximations, it seems to be around 1880. Baba grew up among the trappings of wealth, somewhat spoiled by his uncle Visheshur Nath. He went to school in the family phaeton. He quit school in Kanpur before graduating after a teacher slapped him in class. He never went back. When the family split, he got the short end of the stick- the great room mentioned earlier and the surrounding undeveloped area. The wealth disappeared, but the somewhat haughty demeanor of being born wealthy remained. He never attempted to acquire any means of income. He felt working for someone was below his dignity.

His sister Vilayati was married into a Kapoor family in Kanpur, and I vaguely remember her. But we remained close to her family, and my dad helped her grandson, Rajju bhaiya, get admitted to Agra medical college. I also vaguely remember Baba's mother- Bari Dadda (old grandmother), who died when I was about 4yrs old.

Baba was married at about the age of 14yrs. In Shahjahanpur to Baua, who hailed from a wealthier family. Apparently, a proposal had also come from the maharaja of Burdwan (Kapoor khatris) in Bengal for one of the princesses but it did not work out. The barat (wedding party) traveled by rath (covered wagons drawn by bullocks), then across the Ganga, about hundred and ten miles, about a five-day journey. It stayed in Shahjahanpur for about a week.

Every day the host family got the vegetables and other provisions needed for their guests from the vendors at the market, not paying them, for nearly all were indebted to them. It is said that on the fifth day, they started praying, 'Ya Khuda ye barat kab vapas jayaiygi' (O Lord! Will this barat (grooms party) ever leave?) I did not learn much about Baua's family except that they were 'filthy rich.' It was said that the district Commissioner (head of civil administration and nearly always a British person) wanted some bonds to be sold and asked the family to help. The family bought them all, sending the money to him in large bags of rupee coins on bullock carts. (Money was stored at home as coins of silver rupees in bags). The head of the family was called 'Radhoo Kaanay' (Radhoo the one-eyed), for he was blind in one eye. It was also said that many of his employees and the horse of his carriage were also one-eyed. The family had a tragic ending, with all male members dying young, leaving four generations of widows. All the wealth disappeared between litigation among distant heirs and probate court taxes.

There is a tradition in some Khatris, that during a wedding, the father of the bride asks the groom if there is anything he would like as a special gift and fulfills the wish. Baba was asked, and he replied that God had blessed his family with most everything. Encouraged by the prospect of getting away with not having to give something, possibly expensive, his father -in- law repeated the offer to show his generosity. Baba thought for a moment and said that they had everything except an elephant, so that would be nice. Flustered by his blunder and apparently not willing to give such an expensive gift, his father- in- law handed him a toy elephant! Elephants being expensive, owning one was considered the epitome of wealth. Later, to annoy Baua, Baba would tell this story within her earshot to try to illustrate how cheap her family was!

Baba was poor but proud, which did not help his immediate family any. He started selling some of Baua's jewelry to survive and to marry off their two daughters. They had two girls and two boys. When Baua refused to part with any more of her jewelry, he started selling household items. Part of his pride was never going to the bazaar, as only servants were supposed to go there. It is said he would deform metal utensils and have the servant take them to the bazaar to sell them as scrap metal, so the people would not think the family was destitute and selling household goods.

This was self- delusion based on false pride, as everyone knew what the reality was. Yes! Even poor 'upper-class' people had servants. Next came the mortgaging of the house and property to a merchant in a nearby town.

Baba and Baua had four children. Two boys, Harihar Nath, Kailash Nath, and two girls, Girija and Kaushalya. Girija was married to Mohan Mehrotra in Calcutta and Kaushalya in Kanpur into a Kapoor family. I never saw my aunt Kaushalya as she died young and left an infant, who my grandparents tried to take care of, but did not survive. So I do not know much about her. Baba had few possessions, but some ledgers called 'Bahi - Khata' were among them. These were long, thin papers bound in a red cloth cover and folded in one or two folds. The writing inside was a shorthand form of Devanagari script of Hindi, indecipherable to me, called Muria.

My Mother's Family

My mother's side of the family was seldom talked about.

But this is what I know. They were Mehra (a contraction of Mehrotra) and lived in Shahjahanpur, which was a Muslim majority town. I never saw my grandfather, for he died before I was born. His name was Giasiram, and he worked as a track inspector for the railways. After he retired, he went into business selling cloth for coffins. I have a faint memory of my grandmother from the few times we visited. She was a short woman who was very loving. I called her Nani (maternal grandmother) and never knew her name. I had one uncle, Tulsiram, who I called mama (mother's brother). He was older than my mother. He was a tall man with a long face and a serious demeanor. He knew Urdu and some Persian, which he learned in school. He expanded his father's business and became a jeweler and money lender and acquired some agricultural land (zamindar), and became reasonably wealthy, with a two-storied shop in the main bazaar. He added to the house and property he inherited. The house had a female (zanana) and male (mardana) sections. The female section was the usual Indian style of an open courtyard surrounded by a corridor into which rooms opened. One of the rooms was my Uncle's 'strong room,' which had a large walk -in iron bar cage with a large padlock on it. There was a well in one corner of the courtyard. This was the main section of the house and was used for board and lodging. A few steps up, connected it to the mardana (male section), which had three rooms and a verandah, in front of which was a paved area leading to a garden. It was mainly used in the daytime by my uncle and for entertaining or lodging male guests. The garden was beautifully laid out, with several rows of rose bushes surrounded by jasmine vines. I can still smell the sweet smell of those flowers as I had helped pick some for Nani's puja. On the left side was a bathroom and a well, and at the farthest end, a covered toilet. It was said that an itinerant sadhu, predicted to Uncle that his older son would bring him luck and fortune. Uncle took great care of his older son and named his firm 'Tulsiram Saligram.'

My aunt was small and nondescript, with a throaty voice. I had five cousins, two male, and three female. The oldest was Saligram. He had cerebral palsy but managed pretty well. He was very loving to us, loved tea, made plenty of it in a 'pateeli' (a round metal vessel), and insisted that everyone have it. My uncle had a full-time servant to look after him. The younger son, Shriram, was nearer in age to my sister Vidya Bahen, and went into business with his father after graduating from college. He was soft-spoken and very loving of us. Kamala was the oldest female cousin, the same age as my sister Sidya Bahen. The next one was Vimla, my age, and then Sheela, a few years younger. My last visit there was when I was in my third year of medical college. My aunt, uncle, and cousin Saligram had passed away, and the female cousins were married and moved away. Sriram bhaiya's wife was very good-looking and affectionate. It is unfortunate that I did not get a chance to bond with this part of the family.

Father and Uncle

My father and uncle grew up in poverty. My uncle was two years younger than my father. Once my father finished high school, he wanted to go to college. So he went to Kanpur and stayed with Madanlal, the least estranged of Baba's uncles, and went to Christ Church College. It did not seem to work out after a year or two. He was married to my mother around that time. Since girls were married very young, they generally went back to their parent's house right after marriage and stayed there for six months to a few years. This custom was called 'gawna.' I think my mother's gawna was pretty long as my father was away at college. My maternal grandfather (Nana) supported my father's education, as he transferred to Banaras Hindu University, founded by a progressive Hindu leader- Pandit Madan Mohan Malviya. I think he also got a small scholarship and periodically, some help from the head of a branch of the family settled in Calcutta. He was sent to Allahabad one summer by Pandit Malviya to help Moti Lal Nehru, who was donating his house (Anand Bhavan) to the Congress party. When he found out he was from Kannauj he asked him if he was related to Visheshur Nath and was pleased to know that he was.

He did his post-graduation in Hindi. He also joined law classes and came first in class at the University in the first year of a two-year course. Things were dire at home. My uncle, two years his junior, had been sick off and on, was also married, and lagged behind academically. Everything was mortgaged to the hilt. He decided to drop law and find a job to take care of the family. Pandit Malviya, his mentor, got him a job as a professor of Hindi at St. John's College Agra in the newly opened department of Hindi. Baba was very unhappy about that, for he wanted him to become a lawyer. Also, he told my dad that no one in the family had ever worked for someone else. His pride still came before reality! So the family branched to Agra. It was 1928.

He rented a house in the old city in an area called Moti Katra and brought over his wife and daughter and, a little later, his brother and his wife. His salary was Rs.100/month which was apparently a decent amount at the time. He started saving money and gradually started to pay off the mortgages of the properties in Kannauj.

There was a medical school and a teaching hospital, (Thompson Hospital) in Agra, a stone's throw from where the family lived. It gave a diploma, after a three-year course in allopathic medicine, following high school. Uncle had just matriculated at Kannauj, so dad applied for him and asked him to come down. The selection was after an interview with the principal. The interview took place under a tree on the grounds of the school hostel. The principal, an Englishman, sat under the tree at a desk with the applications and a couple of orderlies helping him. The candidates stood at a distance and came over to the desk for the interview as their names were called by the orderly. After the interview, each candidate was asked to wait on the left or right side, behind the tree. Uncle was directed to the left side. He stood there for a while, then quietly asked an orderly about the reason for separation. The orderly whispered that the ones selected were on the other side. Uncle thought fast, and when the orderly was distracted, slowly moved over to the other side. After the interviews were over, a tally of the selected was made, and it was found that there was an extra person in the count. After further investigation, it was found that my uncle was the extra one! The principal came over and talked to my uncle, who told him he wanted to be a doctor very much. The principal looked him over and decided that a candidate with such determination and presence of mind deserved to be admitted. It also helped that my uncle was a good-looking young man. Such are the vagaries that decide one's fate in life!

My father was different from my uncle in many ways. My uncle was practically devoid of body hair; my father was hirsute. Uncle had short wavy hair- father was bald. Uncle had a ready smile; father had a stern look. Uncle was rarely angry, and father was easily angered, though equally fast to cool down and try to make amends. We grew up respecting our uncle but were not afraid of him. We were afraid of my father. Uncle did not hesitate to show affection within the constraints of contemporary societal norms; father was Victorian. Though there was only a two-year difference between them, my uncle treated my father with the utmost respect. I never saw or heard a single cross word between the two. My uncle never smoked in front of my dad, and dad would not come to the area when he could smell smoke or would announce his presence by speaking louder before approaching the area. When I was older, I came to understand the unstated bond of love between the brothers. Uncle was a very practical man who, while not unscrupulous, did not let minor matters of rules crimp his style. His brother was a stickler for scruples and societal rules, as he saw them. Uncle had the Haveli, which had been locked and vacant for decades and thought to be haunted, forced open, cleaned, and portions rented off. He defied the tradition of not owning a black animal, though he regretted it later. He was enterprising and tried his hand at many businesses. Over the years, he had a perfumes business- 'Ravindra Nath, Surendra Nath,' agency to sell ready- to-wear clothing, agency for Dhariwal Woolen Mills clothing material, selling papier- mache toys at the Ram Lila fairs, dispensing 'medicinal spirits'- in approximate succession; and a pawn business. They were all short-lived, and I doubt if they made any money, except for the pawn business. The pawn business was bizarre. It consisted of a broker bringing a sealed package, the contents of which were unknown, to be pawned for a short term at usurious rates. So the lender had to trust the broker as he did not know what was in the package. He also bought some real estate in the bazaar and had income from rentals in the Haveli and properties surrounding the house.

Uncle had beautiful handwriting. He would write a postcard to my father every two weeks or so. Every part of the card was utilized, including the edges of the area for the addressee with calligraphy grade writing. The post card cost two paisa (1/32 of a rupee), and he got his money's worth! In the great room in Kannauj, he had his own built-in-the wall cupboard where he kept his clothes and money. He would unlock the lock on it with the key hanging from his 'janaiu,' when he came in after the morning clinic, then stack the income in neat piles of coins and notes (bills) in their separate denominations. He kept meticulous accounts. He seldom traveled due to the requirements of his practice, and when he did, it was for as little time as possible. I do not think he had a great desire to do that.

Father (Babuji)

My father's name was Harihar Nath. He was called Bhaiya by his brother and sister and Babuji (father or gentleman) by us, and Tauji (father's older brother) by his nieces and nephews. He was of medium height, light brown skin, strongly built, bald from an early age, imposing, and stern looking. He had a short temper but cooled down fast.

Asides from impressions in childhood and early youth, I did not know my father very well. I learned a lot more in retrospect. He was generous and considerate and helped people throughout his life. He made friends easily and was prescient in many ways. Since he was a professor at a prestigious college, over the years, his protégés were innumerable. He had a large number of friends and acquaintances. There was always a small gathering at our place in the late afternoon and evenings. Some were regulars who came daily. Tea and snacks were offered to some; occasionally, some stayed for dinner. Overnight guests were not infrequent. Relatives, friends, old students, and sometimes there were guests who were friends of friends. It was never asked how long they would stay, but no one took advantage of that. I remember sometimes one or two of his students stayed for the entire summer. Sons of friends from Kannauj stayed for weeks to prepare for tests (pre-med, etc.) Or people just in town for business for a day or two. Nearly all of them had access to the entire house, as only people who were like family were allowed to mingle with the females in a Hindu household. Most were lodged in the corner front room (drawing room) or the 'dining' room.

Sometimes father would give a dinner party for special guests, never less than ten or twelve. I remember when I was ten or eleven, one day, a few men came and inspected the house and the kitchen; and then there was a group of cars and a police car outside our house. Some V.I.P. was coming to our place for lunch. It caused quite a stir in the 'colony' (neighborhood). I later learned that it was a minister of the central government of India who was a former student of my father and wished to see him on his visit to Agra.

He had traveled extensively in India when he was younger, attending the meetings of The Oriental Society, of which he was a member. At the time, not many traveled, for it was not easy to travel; it was expensive and considered a luxury. Tourism was mostly limited to pilgrimages. He had been to the Khyber Pass in the west, to Assam in the east and Shimla in the north, to the tip of India (Kanyakumari) in the south, and places in between.

Ever since he guided his brother through medical education, father seemed to have had an affinity for doctors. Nearly all the doctors of Agra Medical College were either his friends or acquaintances. When someone in the family was sick, we would have a doctor friend come over to see them. There was never a fee charged. I remembered Dr. Varma, an ophthalmologist, coming to our place with an assistant and sterile supplies in a metal container and performing cataract surgery on Baua in our drawing room. The principal of the medical college, Dr. Gaur, was a very close friend of his in the late 1940s and early 1950s. He was also involved, somehow, in the selection process at the medical college, for there was an interview after the written exam. He got Rajju bhaiya (his cousin's son) admitted. Prior to that, it was Girish mama and Padam chacha's brother Akhilesh (Bharosi chacha). I remember that Ravi Bhaiya's age (for some reason deliberately reduced by one year as his official date of birth, from 1930 to 1931) became a problem in being admitted to medical college, for that made him a few months short of 18yrs (the required minimum). Father 'managed' it somehow. When I overheard the conversation about it, I remember saying, "Why don't you make the 1 into a 0." I was obviously chided. Girish mama stayed with us for two academic years while doing his Master of Surgery courses. So for two years, we had our own in-house doctor!

He was not into politics but was a major player in the election of Mr. Mahajan, his Principal at St. John's College, who ran for the provincial state legislature on the Congress party platform. He was also one of the local organizers of the All India Congress Committee and was on its Dias with Prime Minister Nehru one year. He also helped organize the All India Science Congress meeting held at St. John's College in 1956 at which Nehru spoke. I was able to be near the podium because of that and got a closer look at the charismatic Nehru. He was on the Board of Murari Lal Khatri Girls College, Nagari Pracharini Samiti, (Organization for the Propagation of Hindi), various committees of Agra University, and other organizations.

He helped many poor or disadvantaged students get admitted to St. John's College and mentored others. Helped others by getting them admitted to other institutions or getting jobs where his friends or former students were in charge. He helped Padam chacha move out of the inner city by making him buy land in a development near us and build a house there.

Ever since we moved to Civil Lines, he had developed a habit of going for a walk for a couple of miles, early in the morning and after dinner. He had a collection of walking sticks and always took one with him. He had also given up spicy food, so my mother cooked some of his food separately. He had started to have double roti (western-style loaf of bread), cheddar cheese, and Marmite for breakfast in the winter. Cheddar cheese came in tins, imported from Britain. Marmite was a brownish-black spread that came in a bottle that looked like an ink bottle. It had a strong smell and was an acquired taste. He and Girish mama were great devotees of both.

I did not know about his finances but I suspect that he did not have much, for he was salaried, and our expenses were not few. He had some income from examinations and reviewing books, but I don't think it was much. I overheard him mention his salary in 1952 as Rs.450 a month. He was offered the job of Principal at a college in Moradabad; he tried it for a couple of weeks but came back. His was essentially a dead-end job as he came as a Professor and chairman of his department and remained so for his entire career. There was no chance of advancement, as at St. John's, only a Christian could be the Principal. He had students who did their Ph. D under him, but he did not have one himself. So he did his Ph.D. late in his career.

He was a stickler for detail and followed the rules at a time when society winked at rules as mere suggestions. We had a gate with a latch at the entrance to the house. When people came in or left, most would leave the gate open or unlatched. He would make them turn around and latch the gate as they came in or left, in no uncertain terms. For most, it was no big deal; for him it was good manners and a good habit. It became well known that at Tandon saheb's you made sure you latched the gate! It also helped in that it prevented stray cows, dogs, and other small animals from wandering in.

It is both difficult and awkward to try to portray a picture of a person who begot you in a different era, a different society, under different circumstances, and be objective. I have tried. I am certain that under the stern, undemonstrative visage, there was great love and affection for his immediate family in his heart.

Mother (Bhabhi)

My mother was called Bhabhi (older brother's wife) by everyone because we heard my chacha (uncle) call her that. Baua and Baba called her Shahjehanpurwali (one from Shahjahanpur) or Bahuriya (dialect for daughter-in -law). I have described her earlier. She followed all Hindu family traditions to the letter. Her life consisted chiefly of praying and cooking, with other activities interspersed in between. She rarely got angry, raised her voice, or gossiped, to my knowledge. She read the Tulsi Ramayana for an hour each morning and observed all the innumerable festivals and fasts. She was an excellent cook with no written recipes. A sweet smile was her answer to a lot of things. Despite this, she was not a simpleton. She had a wry sense of humor. Once Sidya Bahen, trying to needle her as she was lying on a charpai (cot) sunning in the lawn, asked her, "Who out of your four children do you love most?" "Which of your three children do you love most?" She replied with a smile-silencing her. She was a woman of great fortitude and determination and was well-traveled. She had stayed in Bhopal with Ravi Bhaiya for a while when he moved there. She traveled on a special 'pilgrimage train' all over India with Chachchi, visiting and worshiping at all the major places of pilgrimage. She traveled to the U.S. with my aunt (Chachi) to see her U.S. family in her late seventies. Needless to say, I loved her very much.

Religion, Beliefs, and Superstitions

Hindu religion, one of the oldest in the world, is hard to define, and I will not attempt to, as it is beyond my capabilities. I will attempt an outline. It is basically a big tent in which many forms of belief are subsumed, many contradictory, even from 'revealed' religions, e.g., the Abrahamic religions. Predestination, heaven and hell, rebirth, and rituals are some of its essentials. It is not centrally organized. You are free to believe (Astic) or not believe (Nastic) in God and in whatever form of God you wish. It may extend from God as one (advait), formless and unimaginable (achintya), to animate. Rebirth, based on one's merits and demerits, is a basic Hindu concept. Freedom from that (moksha) and ultimate union with God (Nirvana) is the goal. The world is destroyed and recreated periodically is another belief. A host of mythologies have grown over millennia, with gods, goddesses, and saints. But to give some idea to the uninitiated, the most accepted concept is of God as a Creator (Brahma), Sustainer (Vishnu), and Destroyer (Shiva). Vishnu gradually became the dominant form and incarnated periodically in the world when good was overwhelmed by evil to restore good. (Yada yada hi dharmasya, glanir bhavati Bharata. Abhyutthanam adharmasya tadatmanum srajanmiham) in Sanskrit. Ram and Krishna were His more popular Avatars. It is up to one to believe in whatever one wants to. Non- Hindus find it confusing. But it is what it is.

The two basic texts of modern Hinduism are the Gita (Song), a part of the epic Mahabharata, and the Ramayana, which is the story of Rama. Both written in indeterminate ancient times. Gita is mainly philosophical. Mahabharata is about the great battle between two prominent Aryan clans in North India. Ramayan is more popular, written by the poet

Valmiki with several versions written later by poets in their regional languages. It also extended to Southeast Asia, i.e., Indonesia, Cambodia, Malaysia, Thailand, and Laos, with the Indian conquest, with each developing their own versions. Among the common folk, it is still enacted in drama from all over India. Temples, ancient and modern, are devoted to God in the form of Vishnu (Rama and Krishna), Shiva, and other goddesses and gods. There are innumerable permutations of this religion. Jainism, Buddhism, and Sikhism are its off-shoots, founded by their Hindu dissidents. There is no process of 'conversion.'

Hindus are basically believers. It doesn't take too much to convince them to believe something. I think this is based on an open-mindedness and a "there's no harm in it' attitude than gullibility. Exclusivity of belief is a foreign concept. A Hindu has no difficulty venerating a non–Hindu concept of God. A Hindu would go to a church, mosque, gurudwara, and temple without any compunction. Veneration of holy men and holy sites was common no matter what religion they belonged to. At the level of the rural Indian, whether Hindu or Muslim, going to a site of veneration to celebrate or pray was common. They were usually tombs of holy men (dargah) or their residence (ashram), where sometimes amulets (ganda- taviz) were given for a wish or desire, e. g. for a child or recovery from an illness. One's situation in life and events in life were accepted as the will of God or fate. One's situation in life was often ascribed to sins (paap) or merits (punya) of present or past births. Multiple conquests from the northwest affected beliefs somewhat but were subsumed as the conquerors settled.

Islamic conquest in the eighth century and onwards resulted in conversions, some voluntary but mostly forced, of a sizable population. But by and large, the religions coexisted peacefully. In Mughal times some powerful emperors had Hindu mothers. In my time, strife, in the form of the Hindu –Muslim riots, was incited by rumors or lies deliberately spread by unscrupulous people for nefarious purposes. This and other reasons lead to the partition of India. Into a Muslim nation-Pakistan and the rest- India.

There was a hereditary caste system from the time of the Aryans. There were four castes. Brahmins (priests), Kshatriyas (warriors), Vaishyas (merchants), and Shudras (menial workers). This tradition was passed down for generations till many invasions and constant influx from outside had drastic effects on Hinduism, and inevitably changed it, for better or worse. At one time, Hinduism was practically wiped out by Buddhism, but it revived in the eighth century A.D. and gradually wiped out Buddhism in India while it was spreading outside it. Vegetarianism and non-violence were a few of the many influences it left behind.

There was no formal way of worship. It varied from renouncing the world, meditating and living in isolation, praying at home to religious icons of one's desired form of God, or of any god or goddess of mythology, or going to one or many temples. You could worship on your own or have a priest involved. Reading the Ramayana of Tulsidas, or the Gita. Listening to discourses on them by holy scholars. In our area, an uninterrupted, non-stop, out loud recitation of the Tulsidas Ramayana, by friends and family over twenty-four hours (akhand-Ramayana) was common, especially after a wish was fulfilled. The story of Satyanarain (Satyanarain katha), read by a priest in your home was another form. Singing of bhajans (religious songs) as a chorus to the accompaniment of a dholak (drum), manjira (castanets), and harmonium was common (Kirtan). All pujas ended with the distribution of some sweets in a container made of twig-knitted dry leaves (dona) and a mixture of sweet milk and yogurt with almonds and other nuts in it (charanamrit), in small clay cups (sakora or kullarh).

Hinduism spread, as mentioned earlier, from India to several countries in south-east Asia as the Hindus colonized these regions, and still survives in the tiny island of Bali and in smaller numbers in all of south-east Asia. Vast Hindu kingdoms existed in the area leaving magnificent monuments like Angkor - Wat. Sanskrit's influence is seen in peoples and place names derived from Sanskrit. Hindu names, e.g., Sukarno (good ears), King Bhoomibal Adulyadej (King of immeasurable brilliance), Prince Norodom Singhanuk (Narottam Singh), Singapore (Lion City), and many more, were and are common. In Indonesia, they were the most common, but after the spread of Islam there, they started using Arabic names under Saudi influence in the last few decades. Ram Lila, in dance form, is still a cultural heritage. Its national air-lines is called Garuda after the mythical Hindu bird. Ganesh is depicted on paper currency. But the greatest export of India was Buddhism- to all of Asia except the extreme west.

India's contribution to the world in astronomy, mathematics, literature, medicine, and surgery is varied and significant. The concept of the numeral '0', the longest composition and collection of verse in the world as Mahabharata and Ramayana, many times longer than the Odyssey and Iliad combined, and much more.

At one time, Hinduism was synonymous with vegetarianism. It did not start out that way. Ancient Aryans ate meat. All kinds of it, as written in the Valmiki Ramayana.

With the advent of Buddhism and Jainism that gradually changed, and the majority became vegetarians. Somehow, cows went from being food to wealth and veneration, and cow slaughter became a cardinal sin. The complexity increased as non-vegetarian non-Hindus became a substantial minority and the rulers. It was never an all-or-nothing deal. Hindu Rajput' and others ate what they hunted. Coastal and riverside populations ate fish. So, like Hinduism itself, it became a complex matter, and one saw in it what one wanted to see. But at the time, the vast majority of Hindus were vegetarian.

Hindu society, like most other societies, was male-centric. Polygamy was legal. Women were respected, adored, and even venerated but were not equal to men in society. A girl born in a family, though loved, was no great cause for celebration. She was considered a liability. Her honor had to be guarded (one of the reasons for childhood marriage), a suitable husband had to be found, and dowry had to be given. She was to be part of another family. She had no choice in marriage as it was considered a relationship between two families. (Boys were in the same boat regarding marriage). A girl's birthday was not celebrated. She had no right of inheritance from her parents. All major decisions were made by males. Society had adjusted to and even thrived under these rules. Whether right or wrong by present standards, it is unfair to judge in retrospect. The rest of the world was no different. Only it took longer to change in India.

Superstitions

Superstitions were common. It was considered bad luck to travel east on Monday or Saturday. (Som sanicher purab na chala). It was bad luck to see a one-eyed person first thing in the day, or a cat crossing your path, or someone sneezing at the start of a journey, or to travel in a group of threes. Saturn and Saturday were inauspicious. At Kannauj, a young man from the Taili caste (dealing with oil, massage, and being messengers) would come in the morning on Saturdays with a copper container with mustard oil and a small statue of Saturn in it, as mentioned earlier. We put a coin in it to help ward off evil. Eclipses, mainly solar, were considered harbingers of ill luck. One did not watch them. In Kannauj all the water containers were emptied during an eclipse. I am not sure why. It was a good omen if your right eye or right arm twitched, to see an owl at dawn or a blue-jay at any time.

The twitch omens were reversed for women (left side). When you wished for something and were breathing predominantly through your right nostril, it would come true. One sneeze before the start of a journey by anyone was inauspicious, but two were o.k. A crow cawing on the rooftop indicated the arrival of guests. The first sale of the day at a shop (bawni) must go through to bring good sales for the rest of the day. There were scores more.

Beliefs and Customs

We had a family belief passed down of not owning a black vehicle, animal, or blanket. The story I heard was that there was a satee (a woman who immolates herself on her husband's funeral pyre and is venerated) in the family years ago. Her husband had died after being bit by a black snake lodged in one of his shoes. So she forbade the things mentioned. In our family, the tradition was followed. My uncle chose to ignore it and bought a water buffalo (which was black and yielded more milk than a cow at the time). Soon after, his first wife (Bari chachi) developed tuberculosis and died. No one ever dared to break the taboo afterward. Married Tandon women also did not wear glass bangles. Amulets were given as talismans, as mentioned earlier, at Hindu temples and Muslim shrines (dargah) and were worn around the neck or as an armlet to ward off evil. All young boys in our family wore a thick black thread (kardhani) around their waist, and infants and toddlers had a small black smudge placed on one side of the forehead (kala tika) to avoid getting the evil eye. Admiring the good looks or health of a child in the family was considered a hex or jinx (nazar) and was not done. If an outsider did it, to get rid of any jinx, a small piece of burning cloth was waved around the child (Nazar utarna). A jackknife was placed under the pillow of male infants and toddlers at all times. Shoes were removed before entering the house and any place of worship.

When someone in the family died, all the men had their heads shaved as a sign of mourning. The dead body was covered in a white sheet and placed on a bamboo bier, tied to it, and shouldered by close relatives and friends, chanting 'Ram nam satya hai'-(God is Truth), and carried for cremation on the banks of a river close by, or if there was no river, to a designated site. It was placed on a pyre of wood and then lit by the oldest son, or the oldest son present, or the closest male relative. The ashes were immersed in the river. If possible, some were saved and deposited at a holy pilgrimage place like Allahabad or Hardwar in the river Ganga. On the thirteenth day, a ceremony was held (teraheen), and the family priest or Brahmins were feted.

Shoes were not allowed in temples or at puja and were not worn inside the house in most families. After a religious ceremony or on visiting a temple, men had a perpendicular vermillion mark placed on the center of their forehead. Men covered their heads with a cloth cap (topi) at all pujas (worship). Widows wore white and no makeup or jewelry and, in some communities, had shaved heads. Widow marriage was forbidden. Married women wore a red mark on their forehead (tika) and vermillion powder in the part of their hair (sindoor), bangles on their wrists, a ring/rings on their fingers, and middle toes (bichwa), and silver anklets with tiny bells (payal), or silver rings above the ankle. They always had their head covered with one end of the sari, and pulled it down over the upper part of the face in front of the older males. A single girl could wear all the jewelry except for toe rings and vermillion in the hair parting. Mehndi (henna) was used by women in intricate designs on palms, feet, and forearms as part of makeup at festivals and weddings. Parents and older close relatives of a married daughter did not stay at her place or eat there. If they did, they paid her some money as compensation before departing. When departing after a visit or leaving for a journey, males had a red vermillion tika marked on their foreheads, and the younger males bent and touched the feet of all the elders.

Rites of passage

The birth of a male child was a cause of celebration. It reassured (assuming the child survived) the continuation of the family line and a person to give last rites at death, both of great importance. The family priest made a janam patri (horoscope) calculating the alignment of the planets at the time of birth for both a boy and a girl. It was kept by him and forgotten till the time of looking for a match to find a prospective mate. Birth announcements of boys were sent to relatives, and ladoos were distributed to friends and familyAt the birth of a girl - not so.

Mundan and Janayu (Yagnopavit)

A male child's hair was not shorn. Around the age of five years, there was a religious ceremony with great fanfare conducted by the family purohit (priest), when the scalp was shaved off except for a small tuft at the crown (choti). This was Mundan. Before that, it was sometimes difficult to distinguish between a boy and a girl, for both had long hair, often braided in a single or double ponytail.

The next milestone was the Janayu or Yagnopavit ceremony for males. This marked the start of adolescence, more or less like a Jewish Bar-Mitzvah. This was also conducted by the family purohit and also with great fanfare. The scalp was shaved, an elaborate puja conducted and the janayu, or a circular sacred thread, draped across the left shoulder and hanging near the right hip. This was actually three strands of thick cotton threads. It was not to be defiled by it touching the ground or by urine etc. So in the smaller towns and villages, people wound part of it around the right ear before using the bathroom to prevent it from being desecrated. It was to be worn at all times. At the ceremony, the priest covered his and the inductee's head with a cloth and whispered the Gayatri mantra (a sacred Vedic couplet in Sanskrit) in his ear. This was to be memorized and repeated silently or under the breath at certain pujas and ceremonies. The janayu was to be worn at all times and was a hallmark of an upper caste (Brahmin and Kshatriya). As mentioned earlier, in my family, Uncle and Baba used it as a key-chain, as did others. Baby and I had our janayu around the age of 11 yrs. at Kannauj. We went through the rituals as well as the head shaving. It was in early summer, so when I came back to school, I was not totally bald, saving me from having to give an explanation.

Weddings

In our Khatri community, all weddings were arranged. The choice of seeing the prospective bride by the prospective groom was just introduced. Prior to that, the to-be-wed had no choice. Proposals came, usually through relatives, from the girl's family after the boy was scoped out. Then the horoscope was asked for, and the family priest checked it for a match with the girl's. If there was no problem, a formal proposal was made. Senior members or head of both families met, and if agreed, the boy saw the girl at a third party's place, chaperoned, and if he had no objection, laddoos and some other token were sent as 'rok' (firming the proposal) then a 'tika' (vermillion mark on forehead) was placed on the forehead of the groom along with more laddoos and some money. The number of 'baratis' (groom's wedding party) agreed upon, and the date was set, with the recommendation of the family priests. There were certain auspicious months and others when it was prohibited.

Most of the burden of the wedding was borne by the bride's family, as they were traditionally considered the 'weaker' side in this transaction. We did not have a 'demand' dowry, unlike some other castes. The baratis (groom's party), all males, were treated royally, and nearly all their reasonable wishes were fulfilled. The bride's family's relatives, community, and friends helped them with the needed chores. The groom's family invited important relatives and friends, and it was the custom to be asked more than once and it was considered an honor by the groom's family if they consented. This, at times, caused tension in the community as to who got invited and who did not. All expenses of the invitees, to and from the wedding, were paid for by the groom's family.

The ceremony had been whittled down from a five-day affair to three by my time. The board and lodging of the baarat (grooms party) was paid for by the bride's family. The hosts were very solicitous, and as mentioned, nearly all reasonable demands and expenses for the three days were taken care of. There was some exploitation of this by some baaratis, but a good and reasonable head of the groom's family kept a check and did not let it happen.

The wedding was a very festive, joyous, and often chaotic occasion. Things were lost or misplaced or did not happen as scheduled. But no one complained much. Women sang traditional songs with some infiltration of film music. Older women checked out young men and women as wedding prospects for their or other families. It was the time to show off saris and jewelry and have hands and feet decorated with mehndi dye. At the first day's reception, the older generation women sang old traditional 'Gaali' (mild rebuke) songs directed at the groom's family for taking away their beloved child- all in fun.

Baarat was the wedding procession. It started around twilight, headed by a uniformed wedding band with tubas and drums being the main instruments, playing film music. The groom followed on a mare. He was costumed in a shervani (long coat), 'Churidars' (tight legged pants with transverse creases). 'Safa' (turban), wearing a sword, a veil of jasmine flowers covering his face. He was followed by the baratis decked out in their best. Interspersed were men carrying petro-max lanterns to illuminate all this. The band and the party would stop periodically for the band to highlight a song. A young boy from the family would sometimes sit behind the groom. The bride's side would spray the party with light sprays of scented water- especially in the summer.

The groom dismounted after arriving at the doorstep of the bride's place and was welcomed with waving a lit diya/diyas (oil lamp) in front of the groom, with more songs, and the bride placed a garland around his neck. A variation was for everyone to be seated, then the bride came up to the groom with a retinue of girls and garlanded him. This was Jayamala (victory garland) or Swayamvar (selection by the bride) - two of many forms of the ancient system.

The wedding lasted practically the whole night. It was conducted under a decorated mandap (canopy) with a havan (small central fire) to which ghee was added by the priest periodically, and the recitation of Vedic hymns in Sanskrit. The culmination was kanyadan (the giving away of the bride by her parents), followed by the priest tying a scarf from the groom's waist to the bride's and the couple circling the fire seven times amid more Vedic hymns (fayray). A mutual placing of a ring on a finger was also done. The part in the bride's hair was colored with sindoor (vermillion) by the groom.

Meals were not catered but prepared on premises or nearby by professional cooks called 'Halwais' and served by friends and relatives of the bride's family.

The next day or the day after, the barat left amid a wailing of shehnai (Indian clarinet) music and much shedding of tears and some wailing by the bride's family and friends and the bride. The baratis were given 3, 5, or 7 bartan (metal utensils) and laddoos by the groom's family.

Dress and costumes

Most Hindu men, especially Brahmins, wore a small tuft of hair at the crown of their heads (choti). This custom was on the wane in towns and cities. Women wore their hair long in a braid. Some widows had their hair cut short. Men in some regions of India wore turbans of distinctive colors and had different ways of tying the turban and their lower garment (dhoti, tehemat, salwar). The same applied to how women wore their dhotis and sarees. Most women from western U.P. and Punjab wore salwar (pajama type bottoms) and kameez (long collarless shirt) and lehnga (long skirt). Men wore Kurta or a western shirt, with the Hindus wearing the male dhoti or a baggy or tight pajama (lower garment). Some Muslim men wore a tehemat, a wrap-around cloth from the waist to the ankle. The men not wearing turbans wore a cloth cap, which also varied in shape according to the region. A white Gandhi Cap became popular, especially among politicians. There were some other head covers too-but the custom was dying out. It was such a practical approach to social life. You could tell of mourning (shaved male head), participating in a religious ceremony (tika on forehead), married women (dot on forehead, vermillion in hair part and jewelry) from widows (unadorned and wearing white sari or dhoti), single women (no vermillion in part of hair)), and an approaching woman by the tinkling of her payal (anklet with tiny bells). Most of the time, you could tell who was a Hindu and which region they came from without saying a word. The Achkan and Shervani (long coats), a Muslim heritage, were giving way to western coats.

The most amazing in male wear was the langot. This was a T-shaped male underwear. A wide upper part covered the backside, tied in front with attached strings. The bottom of the T was a long narrow piece pulled forward, covering the genitals going under, then over the tie strings, over itself, and tucked to the back. This complicated thing fell rapidly out of favor when ready-made 'briefs' became available.

Greetings and customs

Younger men and women greeted their elders by bending down and touching their feet and were blessed by a hand placed on their head by the elder– especially if not seeing them for a while and on festivals. Some wished elders respect in words (pai lagain). Hindus joined their palms (Namaste) or repeated 'Ram' or 'Jai Ram ji ki' (victory to Ram) or to Krishna or Shiva, depending on their devotion. Muslims touched their forehead with their right palm in many variations and said 'Salaam' (peace) or more formal Arabic 'as salaam-alaikum.' Sikhs said 'sat Sri Akal' (God is Truth). The tiny Christian community followed the Western time-of-day salutations.

A married woman became untouchable during her menstrual period. She could not cook and could not be touched. Most of the burden of religious festivals fell on women. They followed the Hindu calendar, and kept tabs of the birthdays of males in the family, 'shradh' (death anniversaries of ancestors), days for fasting, and festivals. Most of the fasts were observed by women. These were of several kinds. Total fasting (nirjal), or one where only water was allowed, and one where only a particular kind of food, like fruit or grain (Kutu) was allowed. They maintained the site and worship of the family deity. Women ate after the men. Women did not call or mention their husbands by their first names. 'He,' 'him', or 'the father' of her child was used.

Some Hindu men observed a day of fasting once a week, usually Monday or Tuesday, depending on their devotion to a favorite deity. All Brahmins and upper caste Hindus bathed every day and before cooking and puja.

Birthday celebrations were limited to males. This consisted of a small puja, after which the birthday boy got some money or a ready-made garment- usually an undershirt. Lunch was puris. Gulgulas, (balls of deep-fried sweet dough) were the special treat of the day. If the person was absent, a coconut was placed on the seat at the puja to represent him.

Personal care hygiene and environment

Due to the extensive poverty, general hygiene was poor. As mentioned earlier, begging was ubiquitous. Even then, almost every Hindu, including the poor, took a daily bath despite having to wear the same old clothes again. Deodorants were unknown. This was remedied by the well to-do by wearing perfume or dousing the underarms and body with talcum powder. Soaps had come in vogue, and the common folk used a pinkish-red cake called 'Life-buoy.' More expensive ones were-Lux and Hammam. Pears was an imported brand from the U.K. Undergarments, and some other clothes were mostly handmade, washed at home using the common soap bar called -Sun lite. Men and women used kajal (corylium) or surma for both cosmetic and medicinal purposes. Facial cream was used by some urban women. Afghan and Ponds were the popular ones. The use of rouge or lipstick was very unusual. There were some creams claiming to lighten a dark complexion. Most men wore a mustache of various shapes and lengths. Daily shaving was common in the city with professionals and people with white-collar jobs. A stubble was common among the rest. Beards were uncommon except in sadhus and some older Muslims, who often dyed them red with henna. Men's haircuts and sideburns were short. Women always had a single braid, and single girls could have two, but hair never covered the forehead. Both sexes used hair oil. Coconut oil and others were used with a common belief that it made your hair grow. Later, sophisticated men started using hair-creams like Brylcream. Headgear gradually became less common.

Those who could afford had washer men called Dhobi to come and pick up the cottons and return them cleaned, pressed, and starched. Some people washed their own and used a heavy iron powered by hot coals as a press. Dry cleaning was rare for woolens and smelled of kerosene or petrol for days after coming from the cleaners.

Dental hygiene was taken care of by tooth powders of all kinds in urban areas. A crushed (at one end) Neem stick was used in the rural areas. All kinds of teeth and gum diseases, from halitosis, gingivitis, to early loss of teeth, were common. People chewed pan with or without tobacco powder, which took care of the bad breath but hastened gum and tooth problems. General hygiene and habits were also different. People spat most anywhere when outside and had no qualms about urinating behind a wall or into an open drain on the roadside, in the squatting position. Flies, ants, mosquitos, mice, and other small pests were ubiquitous. Futile attempts were made to reduce mosquitoes by using metal sprayers of DDT called Flit.

In the inner city area, open shallow drains (nali) led to a larger drain (nala) which drained into the closest available running waterway. There was very little refuse (koora). Things were biodegradable, repaired, reused, or recycled. Plastic was not yet commonly used. Undomesticated animals like dogs, bullocks, cows, pigs, goats, and sheep roamed the city, a nuisance, but also took care of edible waste. There was little or no air pollution due to the lack of automobiles and major industries.

Death

Death was, of course, tragic. As described earlier, the body was placed on the ground or floor with the feet oriented to the south. It was tied to a bamboo frame bier completely covered in a white shroud and marigold flowers. And carried on the shoulders of friends and relatives (Uthavani), in a procession, to the shamshan ghat (cremation grounds) amid chanting of 'Ram nam satya hai, satya bolo mrityu hai' (God is true and death is real), which was on the bank of a river and placed on a wooden pyre, the head touched with a pole (Kapal kriya) and the pyre lit by the eldest son or the eldest son present, or the closest male relative. The family came home where the males had their heads shaved and then bathed. On the thirteenth day, 'terahin,' a small feast for Brahmins was held. Infants were consigned to the river. When an older person died (over seventy), small coins were showered on the body during the procession.

Any activity associated with the dead or visit to the hospital required a change of clothes and a bath. A bath before the main meal was mandatory. In some Hindu households, one had to remove all clothing before evacuating the bowels. Water was used for ablution. Before the use of soap became common, clean, dry soil (mitti), or ash (raakh) was used to wash hands and to clean metal utensils and then rinsed off with water. A bath meant rubbing your body with soap and washing it all away with water from a bucket (balti), using a round mug (lota). There were no bathtubs or showers.

Reincarnation

Rebirth or reincarnation was a fundamental Hindu belief. What you came back as after death, depended on the balance of the good deeds and sins you committed. Good deeds (punya) merited being born human again, and sins warranted a non-human form. This cycle of birth and rebirth could be broken by good deeds or extreme devotion- a state called 'Moksha' or Nirvana. We had a brush with 'rebirth' in our family.

Bina, my cousin (my uncle's older daughter), four years younger than me, was very quiet as a child. She began calling her sister 'aapa,' the Muslim term for sister, used other such terms, and would become glum at the time of Ramadan (Muslim month of fasting). Not much importance was given to this. One day, when she was about six years old, she was found at the door of an abandoned house in a Muslim neighborhood, about a mile and a half away from home, by a patient of my uncle, who recognized her. He brought her back. Everyone was shocked. When asked why she had gone there, she said that it was her home and she wanted to go back to her home. A woman had died in that house about six years earlier. She grew out of this. But no one could explain her earlier behavior.

Relationships

In Hindu families, there is an explicit word for each relationship, so there is no guessing like in English, e.g., for uncle- is it father's younger or older brother, mother's older or younger brother, father's or mother's sister's husband? Amongst the immediate family relationships, each relationship is unambiguous, e.g., Grandfather- Father's father is Baba or Dada. Mother's father is Nana. Father's mother is Dadi, mother's mother is Nani and 'Uncle'- is Chacha (father's younger brother), Tau (fathers older brother), Mama (mother's brother) Phofa (father's sister's husband), Masarh (mother's sister's husband). Similarly, for Aunt- Chachi, (father's younger brother's wife) Tai (father's older brother's wife), Bua, (father's sister), Masi (mother's sister) Mami (mother's brother's wife). There is no word for 'Cousin.' Each relationship is defined in terms of primary relationships of grandfather, father, uncles, and aunts, brothers and sisters, which can be confusing to an outsider, e.g. first cousins are' brother' and' sister.' To explain the exact relationship, e.g., an uncle's (father's brother's) son- would be 'chachera' brother, (brother from uncle's side), and so on. What does cause confusion is that except for the primary father and mother, the relationship to a close friend's relatives would be similarly adopted. A friend's brothers and sisters would be addressed as he would address them and his parents became uncle and aunt or as the friend addressed them with the relationship suffix attached at the end of the name, e.g., Padam chacha

Here is an illustrative example. When I was around ten years old, I was traveling by train with Harish Chand baba from Kannauj to Agra. Harish Chand was Baba's (my grandfather) first cousin, his father's younger brother's son. I called him baba as per custom. He happened to be much younger than my Dad- in his late twenties. At a station, he got off to get some tea. An older person sitting next to me tried to reassure me by saying that he would watch me till my brother came back. I told him that he was my grandfather (baba), not my brother. The man was stunned. The amazement and disbelief on his face was obvious. When Harish Chand baba came back, the man asked him if he was really my grandfather. Harish Chand baba explained matters to him.

Fifth Standard

I was now in the fifth standard. The class was small, and so was the size of the classroom. Mr. Galloway was our class teacher. He was a tall, middle-aged Irishman, always dressed in a tie and immaculately polished brown shoes. He was strict, serious, brusque, meticulous, and a good teacher. He lived in the small building to the right at the approach of the school building and did some private tutoring on the side. We had the same subjects as in the fourth standard except for drawing, much to my relief. One day Mr. Galloway chided me – "Tandan, you kachoriwala!" While handing me back my homework exercise book. There was a greasy smudge on the newspaper cover on the book. I remembered why. I had been practicing how to walk while balancing a book on my head and had used that book. In those days, everyone used hair oil. Kachori is a small stuffed deep-fried bread.

We had elocution as a subject and learned to recite many poems by poets from the romantic period and passages from Shakespeare's plays. I came back to school every afternoon to play the sport of the season. What I lacked in size and natural talent, I made up with effort and persistence. I had some competition for ranking in class from a Hindu boarding student named Saluja, but I somehow maintained my top ranking, both in the mid-term and final exams. Drawing, not being a subject, I got all 'A's for the first time.

My younger brother (pet name-Baba), got named Sanjaya (Baba was also a term used for a male child of their employers by servants working in British households). This was a departure from the rhyming names of the rest of us. Ravindra (Ravi), Birendra (Little), Surendra (Baby) and Narendra (Kallo). What led my father to choose that name, I do not know. But I suspect that he had become a little religious and started reading the Gita. The narrator of the Epic war in the book was named Sanjay. Also, Nehru (prime minister) named his second grandson Sanjay about the same time, and Sanjay, as a name for boys, took off.

Baba was an adorable child. Quite a handful and full of mischief. Unlike his siblings, he had no fear of father. My father had also become less volatile. Baba was mischievous-which would have brought swift rebuke in days gone by. He broke nearly all of my father's fancy, Japanese-made, colorful, china dishes. He would take a cup or plate, go to the back of the house and drop it from the ledge into the alley and say, "gayee!"(Gone!), as it shattered. The Choubey neighbors would encourage him, thinking it was cute, and he would bring another one and destroy it gleefully. Maybe he liked the sound of the china breaking! Soon quite a bit of it was gone. When he was four or five years old, he developed a severe eye infection, and both his eyes remained shut for weeks. He would walk around like a blind person. It was heartbreaking to watch. Luckily he recovered. Nina, my uncle's second daughter, was about six months older than him and was in Agra frequently, for she was under the care of a pediatrician for some illness. Baba would quarrel with her and would chase her, saying, "Gina ko maar daloonga!"(I will kill Gina!) He called her Gina.

About this time, we acquired a cocker spaniel cub given to my father by Mr. Mahajan, principal of St John's. The pup was reddish brown, and we named him Fire. It was surprising that my mom accepted him, for dogs were not considered 'clean.' Few Hindu families had pets, especially a dog.

In the neighborhood, we had boys of all ages, from Ravi Bhaiya's to mine- and younger- and we played cricket together in the alley behind the house or on a lot in front of Govind chacha's- place, which was much bigger. We would play in the morning before school or after school and on weekends. There was a Mr. Baliga who lived behind Pathak ji's place, whose servant Mangroo, played with us. In the alley, there was no room to maneuver, and one day I got hit hard on the nose by the ball. I bled from the nose, and it swelled up, and the area became black and blue. In a couple of weeks, the swelling went down, but I had a deep indentation in the upper part of the nose. I am sure it had been broken.

The main road in front of the house went north, slightly uphill, making a bend to the left. To the left was a playground and a huge peepal (fig family) tree of the Normal School. Then there was an English -style thatched roof house (a rarity in India). After that was the huge gate of Avagarh, a princely state's mansion called 'Castle Grant.' Its high boundary wall continued till the road split in two. The left side made a sharp turn. The right continued straight, going over a canal (neher) to Dayalbagh and the Jumna River. In between the two roads was the Civil Courts complex of several buildings enclosed by a low brick wall. The left branch curved past several large houses of smaller princely states on the right and Avagarh mansion on the left. It made a sharp bend going past a stretch of bare ground on the left and on the right a church, with a tall spire and a tin roof (tin wala girja), followed by a plum orchard, a small, boys hostel, and a hill, then joined the Drummond road in front of the jail complex; encircling our development (colony). This road was popular among older people for walks in the early morning and evening as there was hardly any traffic at the time. Most of the traffic in front of our house was because of the civil courts, and once they closed, the road was practically deserted.

I made friends with several boys my age. Naresh and Shanti, being the closer ones. Naresh was good at cricket. Shanti was not into sports. People trying to bicycle to Europe or around the world were in the news. Shanti and I were fascinated. We would read these accounts and take out our atlases and follow their courses. We would also build castles in the air of our own trips and let the imagination run wild, knowing full well that our families would never let that happen. But it was fun.

There was a spate of burglaries and attempts at them in the neighborhood. The older of the young men held a meeting that all of us attended. It was resolved that we would hold a night watch around the neighborhood. Teams were made with schedules and assignments. A group of three or four, including us younger ones, would patrol with staves (lathis) and flashlights. It was fun, staying up late and doing something different. It started in winter, but gradually the enthusiasm petered out after a few months. At Govindji's place, Dadi, his mother, who was in her late eighties, slept in the courtyard and was easily awakened by any noise in the alley outside. When awakened, she would say, "I am awake!" to scare off the potential burglar. One time after hearing her, the person/burglar threw a brick in the courtyard- apparently in frustration of being foiled!

One Sunday morning, we were loitering around near Govindji's place when Ramesh, Pathakji's son, came over and asked us if we would like to go for a car ride. He led us to a pickup near his house, which had its engine running, and we piled up in the back. Ravi Bhaiya was in it too. Ramesh started the pickup and came out of the lane and made a left onto the road surrounding the 'colony' and speeded up. We were enjoying the ride and the rush of the breeze when the turn at the jail boundary wall came up. The turn he made was wide, and we hit the wall at a tangent. All of us tumbled out screaming, and the pickup stopped. Some were crying and looking at their scrapes. Ravi Bhaiya had fallen to the ground; his pajama got caught in and torn by the barbed wire on the fence, stained red from several cuts on one leg. Tewariji, from the neighborhood, who was on his morning walk, saw the accident and Ravi Bhaiya's blood, ran to our house, and seeing my dad reading the newspaper on the verandah, shouted, "Tera ladka mar gaya hai motor say!"(Your son has died from a car accident). My father, stunned, ran out and headed in that direction. He saw Ravi Bhaiya slowly limping home, with me a little behind him, and heaved a sigh of relief. Needless to say, we got an earful. It turned out that Ramesh had found this truck parked near his house with a key in the ignition and decided to take a joy ride. He thought it only fair to invite his friends along. He said that at the turn, he had pulled the steering wheel as hard as possible towards himself to stop the truck! He had never driven in his life! He had no clue where the brakes were! How he managed to get it on the road remained a mystery! Looking at it on a positive note, all of us survived the short trip. Tewariji and my father, who were only acquaintances, became friends. He was a professor of Hindi at Agra College.

Ramesh Pathak was a unique character. He was good looking, likable, and persuasive. He was a little older than the oldest in our group- in his mid-twenties, and interacted with us but was not part of our group. He had roller skates and would skate on the road mentioned earlier. Roller skates were rare, and we were fascinated and jealous. He was academically challenged and had not completed his baccalaureate despite several attempts. There were many stories about him. I will recount a few. Some people traveled by train but did not buy a ticket WT-(without ticket) and had ingenious ways of getting away with it. Ramesh was on one such journey when the ticket checker came into the compartment (car) and asked for his ticket. Ramesh looked at him and said brightly, "Aray, jijaji aap!" (Oh! Brother-in –law, it is you!). The checker, taken aback, was embarrassed to ask him for a definite relationship, as in India, even the wife's first cousins could call one Jijaji, and dropped the subject. Another time he stopped a bicycle rickshaw and asked the driver what he would charge an adult and his son to go to their destination. (Fares were charged and bargained per rider, and children were charged half the fare.) Up to two adults and a child could be accommodated. The rickshaw driver quoted him a fare, assuming the son would be a child. Ramesh asked if the offer was firm, and the rickshaw driver agreed. Ramesh and his uncle boarded. The rickshaw driver balked and said that you told me it was an adult and his child. Ramesh told him, "This is my dad, and I am his son, and you just agreed for an adult and his son's fare. Now get a move on!"

Ramesh's father owned a small building with a few shop-fronts on the road to Dayalbagh. Once, a few of us were bicycling back from Dayalbagh and decided to stop and check it out. Close up; we saw a sign- Dr. Pathak's Clinic, in Hindi. Curious, we entered and saw a table, a chair, a desk, and a bench. Ramesh was sitting in the chair with a stethoscope around his neck and a villager across from him on a chair. He motioned us to the bench. He asked the villager what the problem was and he replied that he had this headache for a few weeks, which would not go away. Ramesh listened calmly, then placed the diaphragm of the stethoscope on the patient's forehead, listened, "Hummed" seriously, took out a small bottle with some pills, and told the patient to take one twice a day. The patient thanked him profusely, paid him, and left. I don't know how we kept a straight face as we watched the drama. There were many other stories.

Sixth Standard

I was now in the sixth standard. My class teacher was Mr. Cornelius. He was a tall, dark Indian Christian with wavy hair and smoked a cigar. He had a gravelly voice and wore double-breasted jackets. He was a good and calm teacher, and everyone seemed to like him. Indian history was introduced that year, and I instantly liked it. The period we studied started after the Muslim conquest of India.

An interesting episode happened in class that year. I think it was during our 'midterm' exam. During the middle of it, Prahalad, a day scholar, disappeared. We learned later that in answer to our English exam, he wrote the word 'Ram' in Hindi in a continuous manner to fill up the answer book, hoping it would be converted to the correct answers by a miracle by Lord Ram. Apparently, it was not the right thing to do in a Catholic school! We did not find out what made him do such an unexpected thing, as we never saw him again.

My routine of coming in the late afternoon to school to play the sport of the season remained unchanged. That year MacDonald convinced me to take part in the Athletic meet. We had an Athletic meet once a year with events like foot races, high jump, broad jump, and pole vault. I was never interested in them. Mac and I took part in the 200 yards run, and we came in second and third. I was delighted to get a small cup as a prize. My sole accomplishment in athletics! I still lacked self-confidence and would tell classmates that I didn't think I did well after exams, and they would say that I always said that. I managed to maintain my 'A's and ranking of first in class.

That year my cousin Shri Ram bhaiya got married. He was my mother's brother's son. The wedding party traveled to Shikohabad, a small town not far from Agra, with a large glass industry, of which bangles were the main product. The highlight of the event was my seeing a mujra. Mujra was a gathering of wealthy men, where songs and dances were performed for their enjoyment by women who were hereditary entertainers. I had seen them in movies but never live. The patrons sat on thick cushions leaning back on large round pillows around a carpet, which was the stage. Musicians would sit to one side with their instruments. The performer would come and bow and do salaam (bend slightly and touch her right palm to her forehead) and start to sing and dance or dance to a song sung by another woman in the orchestra. The songs were verses from romantic Urdu poetry. The audience applauded if they enjoyed the performance by exclamations of words of appreciation like 'wah wah,' bahut khoob,' 'subhanallah,' and others (hard to translate), at which time there would be more salaams from the dancer, and patrons would hand over money to the dancer. Some dancers would sing right in front of a particular patron if he was more generous. There were many musical instruments, but the tabla and sarangi (a violin–like instrument) were essential. Pan, tobacco, and sometimes alcohol were served. The session could last all night. It was a dying form of entertainment, a remnant of earlier times. I don't know how I sneaked in, for children were not allowed.

My father used to get answer books to be marked for Intermediate, bachelors, and master's examinations from various boards and Universities in north India right after the finals. They arrived as parcels of various sizes wrapped in a cloth called 'markeen.' The seams were stitched and sealed with stamped lacquer. On the front page of the answer book, was the roll number of the candidate with boxes underneath for the marks to be awarded for each question, and then the total of all that in the last column. My father would examine and award marks inside and then enter them on the front page and tally the total. Then it was re-entered on a separate paper called the 'mark sheet.' All this had to be double-checked to avoid errors. For this work, my father recruited me and the neighborhood boys from the Choubey Ji and Chaturvedis, older than me. I don't know what the incentive was, but they all worked in the afternoons. Then the answer books and the mark sheets were re-packaged in burlap. All seams were sealed with lacquer embossed with my father's seal and taken to the post office to be mailed back. I remember some of the 'markeen' from the parcels being used by my mother after removing the lacquer and making my summer shorts and tops when I was younger. But they still had the seal markings on them! It did not bother me.

Agra University held its annual convocation in Hewett Park outside its offices, under a huge tent. It was an all-day affair, with hundreds of graduates from its far-flung affiliate colleges coming to receive their degrees. I enjoyed going there. My father was always there in some official capacity. It was a grand spectacle with students dressed in black gowns, tasseled mortar boards, and different color ribbons receiving their diplomas. The governor of the province was the Chancellor and was always there. There was also a famous person invited who was the recipient of an honorary award and the honored speaker. To this day, I remember the vice- chancellor saying, "By virtue of the authority vested in me as the Vice-chancellor of this University, I confer upon you the degree of (their degree) and charge you throughout your life to prove worthy of the same"

Diwali

Diwali, the festival of light, was the biggest celebration each year. We waited for it eagerly and with great excitement. The houses underwent a thorough cleaning, and rooms were whitewashed. The bazaars were crowded and humming with activity as it was the time to buy presents, clothes, utensils, toys, decorations, and sweets. We could not wait for it to arrive. It started with buying a hathri. A hathri was usually a small replica of a house with a parapet and a flat roof, made of baked clay and came in many sizes, from simple to fancy. In our house, it was placed in the corner of the main room- mom's room. On it were placed the statues of Lord Ganesh, the god of the initiation of everything, and Laxmi, the goddess of wealth. Several small diyas (baked-clay bowls with mustard oil and a wick for lighting) were placed near it with the paraphernalia of puja (worship). Sweets were exchanged with friends and neighbors. My mother made most of the sweets we used. Gujiyas -pierogi shaped sweets filled with 'khoya' (condensed milk) and raisins, fried in ghee or syrup). Laddoos and barfis (another sweet) of many kinds. We bought some to supplement the sweets we gave away. For businesses, it was the start of a new year, closing the old and starting new account books. The festival lasted five days.

The first day was Dhanterus, when the hathri lamps were lit. A metal utensil was purchased and placed near the hathri. On that day was the main trip to the bazaar, festively lit, decorated, and bustling with crowds, to buy sweets, toys, and gifts. The second day was choti (little) Diwali. We bathed with hot water using 'Batna,' a thick paste of turmeric, and sandalwood oil, in a mustard oil base, as soap. Mother would wave a bunch of twigs doused in mustard oil around our heads while saying, "Anja jhali rog dhog lai jai Diwali " (may Diwali take away all illness and discomfort). A puja ceremony was again held at the hatri in the evening.

The third day was Diwali- the main day. Merchants did puja at their place of business and started new account books, as mentioned earlier. The goddess Laxmi (goddess of wealth) was worshiped. Sweets were distributed and received. People wore new clothes. Preparations were made for lighting the diyas on roofs. We had the kumbhar (potter) deliver diyas. These came in many sizes and were made of baked clay. The ones we used were shallow, palm-sized, round containers. We filled them with mustard oil and placed homemade cotton wicks sticking out at one edge, arranged them in round thalis (trays), and took them to the roof, where we placed them on all the parapets, evenly spaced, ready to be lit. Right after puja, we would go back to the roof and light a Diya and then use that to light up the rest. The entire neighborhood did the same, and soon the dark night would be filled with dancing, flickering lights in every direction, creating a spectacular festival of lights- Diwali! Everyone gathered at the hathri, and the goddess Laxmi was worshiped. There was a Dr. Mehrotra, a native of Kannauj, who lived nearby. He came to the puja like a member of the family. He was younger than my father and was considered and called Chachaji (uncle). Red vermillion mark was placed on the forehead of everyone in descending order of seniority. Younger males touched the feet of all elders and were blessed by them. Children got gifts, usually rupee coins. A special dinner followed. A light was left lit in every room of the house. There was a tradition of gambling on Diwali in some communities. In our family, family members and close friends would sit and play a card game of Flush (like poker). Stakes were low, kidding around and conviviality more. We would (of all ages) play at home or at a neighbor's in the afternoons and at night.

The fourth day was Parva. It celebrated the saving of Mathura from destruction by a rainstorm and flood by Lord Krishna, who held up a hill over it as an umbrella. A small puja was held in the courtyard, and we ate Halva (wheat flour roasted in sugar and ghee with raisins, pistachio, and cashew shavings).

The fifth day, Bhaiya Duj belonged to the sisters. Sisters put a 'teeka' (vermillion mark) on their brother's foreheads and something sweet in their mouths and got gifts (mostly money) from them. The usual puja was held. That completed the festival of Diwali.

The Chaturvedi family behind us moved away and was replaced by the Kapoors, who had fled from the Punjab during partition. The father was middle aged and everyone called him 'papaji' his wife was 'Bi-ji.' They had two daughters and a boy whose pet name was Kukku. Kukku was about 3 years old and would come over very often. He became very fond of Ravi bhaiya. Biji was an excellent cook and a loving host. We enjoyed her parathas and saag frequently. We became like family. And later, actual family, when my cousin Narendra was married to their second daughter- Suveera.

Seventh (Actually Eighth) Standard

I was now in the seventh standard. This was also a transition from childhood to early adolescence. We were allowed to wear long pants in school and use a fountain pen. The seventh and eight standards were combined as we had a total of only fifteen students, including both, in a larger rectangular classroom. Mr. Eastman was our class teacher. He was a slender middle-aged Anglo Indian, wore thin-rimmed round glasses, and seldom smiled. Always dressed in a jacket and tie, he was an excellent teacher, played hockey and football with us after school, and was good at both. He had a large scar on the back of his right hand and the inability to form a fist, so he was essentially left-handed. Rumor had it that he shot himself after a tragic romance.

My stay in the seventh standard was brief. One day my friend and classmate Mac (MacDonald) told me that he was in the eighth standard. This was quite a surprise. I was a little jealous and puzzled. This meant he would be in a different classroom next year. We had been good friends and classmates since the second standard. I knew that 'double promotions' (skipping a class) were awarded rarely, and to very good students. Mac was a good student, but it was I who had consistently come first in class. For the first time in my life, I approached my dad and explained the situation to him.

He did not say much. The next day he gave me a letter to be delivered to the Headmaster- Mr. Merriman. I do not know what was in it, but a day later, Mr. Merriman called me into his office and told me that I got a double promotion and was now in the eighth standard. I was delighted. I let Mac know about it. Nothing changed. We had the same class, books, and teachers. The final exam in the eighth was going to be for the Cambridge University Overseas Junior School Certificate.

On the 26th of January 1952, India became a republic with much fanfare and celebration. The Governor General, the nominal head of government, was replaced by a President with a parliamentary form of democracy.

Hindi was introduced as a 'second language' subject in school that year. It met some resistance from the Anglo-Indian students initially, but soon they reconciled to it. Surprise of surprises! Padam chacha became the Hindi teacher- as Mr. Agarwal! I had a slight advantage in class because I already knew how to read and write Hindi, and it was my native tongue. We had to memorize several poems and write short essays. Jhansi-Ki Rani (Rani of Jhansi) was one such poem, and I remember most of it to this day. I maintained my mischievous behavior with Padam chacha as much as I could respectfully get away with. Once, we were asked to write a short essay on the President of India, Dr. Rajendra Prasad, after he taught us his biography. The President, in India, is mostly a ceremonial position, with the day-to-day governance by the Prime Minister. I wrote, 'The President has no work except for inaugurating events and cutting ribbons at ceremonies, with the result he has gained considerable weight as is obvious by seeing his pictures before and after his election.' It was actually the result of the medicine (cortisone) he was being given for his asthma. I and the public did not know that at the time. Besides, it was disrespectful. But it was true, so I got away with that.

Science, as a subject, also started that year. It was physics and chemistry. The classroom was an amphitheater and a large long lab with faucets and sinks, burners, scales, and bottles with chemicals- to its left. The teacher was Mr. Sharma. He was an older Indian who had been there for a long time. He dyed his hair poorly, as we could see patches of gray hair at the back of the head. He was a quiet man but a good teacher.

By now, all my day-scholar friends were bicycling to school. I had been using Ravi Bhaiya's bike to do chores and graduated from driving ' scissors' style to now being able to ride normally with my feet barely reaching the pedals.' Scissors' style is when you ride standing with one foot on one pedal with the other going to the other side under the bar, so you can only half-pedal, as in the motion of a pair of scissors. It was awkward and difficult, but you could move! But it was also embarrassing when you were no longer a child. Sidya Bahen was one of the few who could speak to dad directly, so I worked on her to try to persuade him to get me a bicycle. New or used, I did not care. I also complained within his earshot how all my friends had bicycles except me. It must have worked, for one day, he said we would go to buy one. I was overjoyed.

We went to Sadar Bazar to a bicycle dealer well known to him and related to Nemi chacha. We were welcomed and offered tea. My father explained to the owner that he was looking for a bicycle for me. He looked at me carefully and showed dad several makes and models of shining, spanking new bicycles in the showroom. He recommended a 24". I was not familiar with the sizes. I rode the one he pulled out a few feet and, in my eagerness, said it felt good. My dad looked around, talked to the man, and chose a B.S.A. Nearly all bicycles were imported from Britain, assembled in India, and relatively expensive. They had no gears. The sole Indian made was called 'Hind' (a contraction of Hindustan), looked a little crudely made as compared to the others, was cheaper, but did not have a good reputation. I only knew of Raleigh, Rudge, and B.S.A. (British Small Arms) brands, though there were more. He asked about the accessories, which were- a light, bell, stand, carrier, tool box, hand pump, mudguard, and lock. My dad chose a bell, a carrier above the back wheel, and a stand. The bicycle would be assembled and ready in a couple of days. We went back to pick it up. I looked at the bicycle. Shiny, brand new, and my own! I was in seventh heaven. I rode it back the four miles home as if riding on air.

A bicycle was a prized and essential possession. It was the most common form of transit. People rode it solo, with a passenger riding side-saddle on the front bar or/and in the back. With bags hanging from the handlebar, with containers tied on the back carrier. Newspapers, milk, produce, you name it- the bicycle transported it. It also spawned repair shops, where a broken chain, a mangled wheel, and other repairs could be made. But the most common one was the puncture and burst repair place, due to the rough and often unpaved roads. They were ubiquitous. At nearly every intersection or corner or sidewalk, under the shade of a tree, even on remote roads. All that was needed to set up shop was a small basin of water, rubber patches, pliers, a pump, and a wrench. The sign for the place would be a used tire hanging from a branch or a ledge. In the evening, the repair man would gather everything up and walk home, for he could not afford a bicycle!

The school was starting to grow in enrollment at the level of K. G. (Kindergarten) and lower standards. K.G. had now expanded from the main building to the one where Mr. Galloway's apartment was. There were more students in the first and second standards, all day-scholars, and overwhelmingly non-Christian. There were many reasons for this, some mentioned earlier, but now gaining more urgency and momentum after independence. An English medium Christian school was considered to have a higher quality of education. There were more people making more money, realizing that their children needed to have a good education to be competitive for good professions and jobs. The importance of proficiency in English was also recognized. My brother, too, got admitted to the school, and after I got the bicycle, I brought him to school on it.

The school was also an orphanage, as mentioned earlier. But now, there were only a few orphans living there. It had a printing press on the left side of the main building, and the orphans helped out there. Mr. Merriman used to make rounds in the verandahs, past every classroom, nearly every period. To go get a drink of water or go to the bathroom, you had to get permission from the teacher. The faucets were across from the ninth-tenth classroom, but the bathrooms were more distant, across the playing field in the back. A senior student, usually in the tenth, and one with a watch, would ring the bell for class periods, short and lunch intervals, and the end of school. The short period was ten minutes in the morning and lunch for forty-five minutes at noon. In late spring, till the summer vacation, the classes started at seven in the morning and ended around noon. Unlike other schools, we had only 'half-day' sessions on Saturdays. The first period was catechism. Non- Christians were exempt but had to come to school at the opening time and spend time in the study hall or on a bench, reading or doing school work. The social life of the 'boarders' involved socials with the girls at the adjoining St. Patrick's. Girlfriends were made and talked about, notes exchanged, and romances bragged about after a few hours of supervised socializing. I never found out what really went on, for I was never invited or attended one. Neither was any other day scholar.

Mr. Eastwood started a classroom wall newspaper. It was on the long wall of the room. It consisted of short articles, school news items, riddles, cartoons, drawings, clippings from newspapers and magazines, and any other thing the class and Mr. Eastwood wanted to be pinned to the wall. The content changed every week. Everyone in the school was welcome to see it. It was very popular.

Newspapers and Magazines

The Indian news and literary Industry was large and thriving, mostly as newspapers and magazines, both in regional languages and English. It was the main form of getting local, regional, and world news. There were regional and national daily papers. The leading ones in English were Hindustan Times, Statesman, Times of India, National Herald, Pioneer, Amrita Bazar Patrica- in North India, and the Indian Express and The Hindu in the south. They followed the British tradition in language, style, and format. There were political cartoons and scholarly editorials. Sunday editions were large and had comics. I remember Maggie & Jigs and Prince Valiant. All in black ink and on relatively coarse paper. Hindi papers were Hindustan and regional papers like Amar Ujala, Ujala, Sainik, and Jagaran. Comic books, all imported, in English, were popular in our school. I recall the Tarzan series, The Lone Ranger, and Hopalong Cassidy. Some classic books were also sold in the 'comic' form, e. g. Hamlet and Julius Caesar.

I was very much interested in and followed Indian and international politics and news by reading newspapers and other magazines. Sometimes there would be discussions of these events at home with Padam chacha, who was also an avid follower of politics and world news. I knew the names of the leaders of most major countries in the world as they seemed very charismatic. Truman, Eisenhower, Rockefeller, Dulles, Peron, Batista, Pearson, Diefenbaker in the Americas, Stalin, Molotov, Beria, of the Soviets, Churchill, Atlee, Bevan, Eden of U.K., Mendes- France, De Gaulle of France, Conrad Adenauer and Willy Brandt of Germany, Franco of Spain, Salazar of Portugal. Ben Guerin and Mahmood Abbas. King Faisal of the middle-east, Chiangkaisheck, Mao, Chou-en lai of China, Tito, Nasser, Nehru, and Sukarno of the 'Neutral' countries. Jomo Kenyatta, Gen.Smuts, Mandela, Nkrumah of Africa. Bao Dai of Vietnam, Norodom Singhanuk of Cambodia, Bhumibal Adulyadej of Thailand, and Hirohito of Japan. Wars were going on against the colonialists in Kenya, Malaya, Vietnam, Algeria, and elsewhere. The Suez Canal was nationalized, causing a mini-war. The Korean War was raging.

The world was divided into two major camps. U.S. and allies, and the Soviet Union and allies, each sabotaging the other and trying to spread their influence. The U.S. had alliances like S.E.A.T.O., N.A.T.O. (South and North Atlantic treaty organizations), and C.E.N.T.O. (Central European Treaty Organization) to contain the Soviet influence. The Soviets had their own cabal. They were overlords of nearly all of eastern and central Europe behind what Churchill called an 'Iron Curtain'. They also had communist parties all over the world. In Italy, France, and Greece, communists were a major political party.

In India, the Kashmir war with Pakistan was festering with lengthy, drawn-out arguments in the U.N. between Zafarullah Khan of Pakistan and Krishna Menon of India. There was a separatist rebellion going on by the Nagas in Assam. India, though 'neutral' in world politics, was being socialized by the nationalization of nearly everything. There were dozens of national and regional parties. Large provinces were being broken up based on regional languages. Major parties split as politics was becoming based on caste, creed, and religion. The 'lower castes' united under the banner of 'Dalits' under B.R. Ambedkar, with demands of 'reserved' rights and preferences and compensation for past wrongs. The Sikhs, led by Master Tara Singh, wanted their own state. Corruption was becoming endemic and bold. The communist party split into Marxist-Leninists, Maoist, Indian, and Trotskyists. The socialist idealism of Nehru was unraveling as it did not thrive on the soil of feudalism and colonialism of a thousand years or more. Pakistan was in turmoil because the smaller eastern section, which was more than a thousand miles away from the western part, had a larger population and a different language and felt underrepresented and discriminated against. While not quite totally understanding the geo-political situation, I was fascinated, for politics, history, journalism, and English literature were my favorite interests.

Corruption

Corruption exists everywhere in the world but gradually became part of the nature of things in India. The reasons were too many, and not possible to speculate here. For the longest time, the judiciary, military, and higher echelons of government remained untainted, but gradually these too succumbed. Bribes seemed to be accepted as part of doing business. When people asked about your income, it was openly a two-part question. Regular salary and 'oopery amdani' (over and above that).

Bureaucracy

A large, unwieldy, sloth-like bureaucracy perpetuated under British rule, engulfed the nation like an octopus. Without going through it, nothing seemed to move, and it seemed to enjoy crawling as slowly as possible. There was more emphasis on following real and imagined rules to the letter than using commonsense and moving things forward. Files grew, things were required in duplicate, triplicate, stamped, and things had to clear an amazing maze of rules and departments. Add to it the bribes and corruption. In retrospect, it seems amazing how anything even worked.

Obviously, it did, but at the cost of markedly slowing down change and progress

I maintained my class position at the mid-term exam, and we started to study seriously and practice for the Junior Cambridge exam. I do not recall the details, but after the exam, that December, everyone said they did well. Our school did have a good reputation among the province-wide Board of our system of schools. When we came back after vacation for the next academic year, everyone had passed with good grades. I came in fourth in the entire province and was awarded a two-year scholarship of ten rupees (about fifteen cents) per month for two years. I was happy and proud when I told my family about it. They were happy for me, but there was no great celebration.

Prithvi Theaters- a touring theater company founded by the famous stage and screen actor Prithvi Raj Kapoor visited Agra. The entire large entourage was lodged in the Normal School next door to us. They staged their plays, Pathan, Diwar, and others, at a local movie house called the Taj. The entourage included Prithvi Raj's father, an imposing retired superintendent of police, and sons Shammi and Shashi. My father invited Prithvi Raj for tea. More than fifty other people, including local journalists, showed up. He was an incredibly handsome and charming person who mesmerized the audience with some anecdotes about his life. At the time, his older son Raj was a rising movie star who made a string of popular movies with a pretty Muslim actress named Nargis. There was a notion in society, due to the frequent romances shown on screen, that the artists had 'poor morals'. There were rumors that, like some other people in the film industry, they were having an affair. A local journalist asked Prithvi Raj, "You are a respectable man, but your married son is having an affair with an actress, what do you have to say about that?" Without batting an eye, he replied, "I am the son of a respectable person, so I have to be respectable, but Raj is the son of an actor, so what do you expect of him?" The cheeky questioner was silenced amidst thunderous applause. Our family got complimentary tickets for the show 'Pathan'. I was amazed at the beautiful production, for I had never seen anything like that before.

I have mentioned earlier that we played cards (gambled) with family and close friends during the Diwali holidays for small stakes and fun. We played a game called 'Flush'. We would play mostly at our place and occasionally at the neighbors, in long sessions, especially at night. There was a lot of kidding, complaining, arguing, and fun, and the stakes were small. One night we met to play at a neighbor's (Brahma Dutta), who lived in a room behind his brother's small general merchant store on the main road. Our ages ranged from mine (14yrs) to Ravi Bhaiya's (22yrs). We sat in two groups on the floor after dinner and were having fun and lost track of time. Suddenly we heard shrill whistles from the road, then a loud banging on the door. "Police! Open up!" We froze with fright, and Brahma Dutta got up and opened the door. Two constables came in. "You are gambling," one said, then ordered us all out and said they were taking us to the police station (Hari Parbat) to be locked up. We were stunned. Some of us started crying, and one or two pleaded, to no avail. It was about a fifteen-minute walk to what felt like an execution. When we arrived at the station, the sub-inspector in charge asked one of our captors what was going on and was told that we were gambling at the Bima Nagar colony. He came out and looked at us and reprimanded us in a loud voice, and asked our parents' names. "Lock them up!" He said as we cowered. A few minutes later, we saw Choubey ji (Govind chacha) walk in. He went to the side and talked to the officer. "Let them go!" The officer said after the brief talk, and markedly relieved, we meekly walked out with our savior, who chided us all the way back home.

Gambling was illegal. Authorities overlooked small family fun like ours when done in private. We were roadside, in a room, which like most rooms in houses, was not soundproof. It was late at night (around 1 a.m.), we were loud, the voices carried, and we were heard by the police patrolling the area. That was our undoing. Someone had seen what was going on when we were marched to the police station and went to Govind chacha's place and reported the matter. All of us were also reprimanded by our parents. It was an experience to remember.

Habits - Good and bad

Pan. Pan or betel leaf chewing was common. It came in many varieties- Desi, Bangla, Maghai, Benarsi, and others. It was brushed with thin chuna (calcium hydroxide) and catechu paste, a few diced supari (areca nuts), and folded in a triangle or cone. Things like finely shredded tobacco, cardamom, peppermint flakes, cloves, and many other things could be added to make it fancier. The older generation, like my Baba, prepared theirs from scratch, with each ingredient in a separate container and the pan leaves wrapped in a wet cloth to prevent drying. But more common was buying one or two from the panwala shops, which were practically at every corner and crossroads. These shops were generally small, with the panwala sitting cross-legged on a small board surrounded by his paraphernalia. There was usually a large mirror, a radio blaring Indian film music, and a few pictures of the Indian revolutionaries like Subhash Bose and other national leaders. They also sold cigarettes and biris as a pack or single, and the larger ones sold bottles of soda, lemonade, and ice in summer.

Smoking, Alcohol, Beverages, and Drugs

Biri was about a two-inch in size, conical, dried, tendu leaf with tobacco in it and a thread tied over the area where the tobacco ended. It came in a thin conical paper bundle and was mostly smoked by the poorer class. The common brands were Pehalwan Chaap (wrestler brand) and Chotabhai Jethabhai (younger & older brother). Cigarettes, filterless, came in hard packs of ten and varied in price with the brand. Common brands were Passing Show, Charminar, Scissors, Red and White, Capstan, and Gold Flake. Panama came in a soft packet of twenty. They were more expensive than the biris. Higher-end brands like Three Castles, Carlton, and 555 came in tins of fifty and were sold in high-end tobacco shops.

Poor people and farmers also smoked the Chillum, a short conical baked clay gadget. Hookah with a short stem was also used by them. Ganja (marijuana), Bhang (cannabis), and Charas (hashish) were sometimes smoked in the chillum and the hookah.

Alcohol was not very prevalent, except among the very wealthy who drank Western alcohol, and more common among the poorer classes who drank Tari (from the toddy) or Tharra (from molasses). Alcohol was a social and religious taboo, and no one drank it openly. Bars existed only in Western-style hotels and some restaurants. There were a few places that sold both foreign and Indian kinds.

Tea was the commonest drink, and people drank it at all times of the day and was available at all times of day nearly everywhere. At home and at work. It was always drunk hot with milk and sugar and from tea stalls in a baked clay container (kularh), which added an earthy flavor and aroma to it. Sometimes it was brewed with Indian spices like black pepper, ginger, or cardamom. Coffee was not very common and was an acquired taste. There were very few restaurants, and the term 'hotel' was used for them, and the food there was considered inferior in taste and quality to the one at home. Indian fast foods like Bhalla (sautéed potato patty), Pani Batasha (mini puris filled with thin spicy sauce), and Cholay (spicy cooked chickpeas) were available on push carts and small shops in bazaars and were popular. Lassi (yogurt drink) was popular in the summer. Soda water, and lemonade were sold in returnable glass bottles with a glass marble at the neck of the bottle. Milk was always drunk hot, and when at a sweets shop (halwai), it was frothed up by dropping it from a metal container in one hand stretched all the way up, into another in the bottom hand and then alternating, till a thick froth (jhag) formed.

Hard drugs (hallucinogenic) like opium existed but were rarely used, and the users were mostly known as 'afeemchi.'

Health and Medicine

Extreme poverty, poor hygiene, and poor diet, all inter-related, resulted in the frequency and predominance of infectious diseases and epidemics, high infant and maternal mortality, and low life expectancy. Malaria, measles, malnutrition, poxes, typhoid, cholera, polio, tuberculosis, leprosy, and trachoma were the common scourges. These lead to immense misery of disability, deformity, disfiguration, blindness, and death. Nearly all hospitals, all in larger towns and cities, were government owned and free to the public. Allopathic-trained doctors practiced in towns and cities, and none in villages. Indigenous medicine, Ayurvedic (vaids), Hakims (Unani system), Homeopaths, Jarrahs (bone and musculoskeletal fixers), and outright quacks practiced with sizable followings with no apparent license enforcement. At home, folk medicines like gul banafsha (sweet violet), inhaling eucalyptus oil fumes from a hanky, salt water gargles- for colds, tulsi-ka karah (basil extract) for malaria, poultices of neem and belladonna for boils, panna (soup of green unripe mangoes) for heat stroke, surma (antimony powder) to the inner part of the lower lid and squeezing the skin of tangerine peel on to the eyeball were a few of innumerable folk remedies tried before calling in a medical practitioner. Most doctors of all stations made house calls.

Ninth Standard

I was now in the ninth standard. We had about fifteen boys in the joint class of ninth and tenth. The room was of medium size and had a large blackboard on the front wall. Our desk assignment was by Mr. Merriman, who was also our class teacher and the headmaster. The subjects were tougher now. Algebra, Geometry, Trigonometry, Science, English, History, Geography, and Hindi. Mr. Merriman was short, slightly chubby, bald, Anglo-Indian, and wore pince-nez glasses and bow ties. He lived in a cottage on the road to the school, in the Church complex, about an eighth of a mile from the school. He rode his bicycle to school wearing a clip on the pants leg of his right ankle and parked it under the porch outside his office. He was serious, and I never saw him smile. Everyone was afraid of him. He taught us math and was very strict and an excellent teacher. Mr. Cornelius taught us History. Mr. Eastwood, English and Geography.

Two new boys joined our class that year. One in the ninth and the other in the tenth. They were Maharajay and Rajay Tandon, two brothers who had come over from Fiji. Rajay was in the tenth, and Maharajay in the ninth. They had an Australian accent, for which they were razzed for a while. Maharajay played hockey with us and was initially polite, saying "sorry" even when he was hit in the shins on purpose by us, till he got wise about it and gave as good as he got. He started attending the catechism class.

Mr. Merriman gave a lot of homework, and used to check it very thoroughly. He made us do problems in algebra and geometry on the blackboard, making sure that we had done our homework and not cheated and copied from someone. In geometry, we had giant protractors, rulers, compasses, dividers, and T-squares, to do the problems on the board. Everyone grumbled about it, some did copy from others, but we did it. In algebra, we had a thick book titled 'Elementary Algebra" by Hall & Knight, and we would get a whole chapter at a time as homework. One day, in Algebra class, Shankar, of the tenth standard, stood up, holding the book, and said to Mr. Merriman, "Sir, if this is elementary Algebra, I would like to see what advanced Algebra is." We did not know what came over him to be so frustrated. Mr. Merriman turned beef-red and said, "Oiy!" halted a bit, then shouted, "MacDonald bring me my cane!" Mac got up sheepishly and left to get it as Mr. Merriman fumed, Shankar stood terrified, and the rest of us sat dazed. Mac came back with the thinnest cane, trying to help lessen the trauma to Shankar's bottom. Mr. Merriman looked at it, took it, and let Mac have a few strikes on his bottom, went back to his office and came back huffing, with the one suiting his rage, and let Shankar have it. No one ever dared to question his authority. Shankar was an orphan who lived at the school.

Mr. Eastwood made subjects very interesting. In English composition, while teaching us how to write a story, e. g. a mystery, he would start with, "It was a dark and stormy night", then ask each student to stand up and add a few lines, and soon we had a story. Grammar was another matter. Our textbook was- Nesfield's Grammar. No matter how interesting Mr. Eastwood tried to make it, I had a mental block for it and hated it. We also had Silas Marner and Julius Cesar and Anthology of English Poems, predominantly with the poetry of the Romantic period. I loved poetry and memorized quite a bit of it. I wrote several short stories and poems, but mercifully they did not survive.

Mr. Cornelius taught us history. We had Indian history, from the Muslim conquest of India to the British period. My favorite was the Mughal period. I was moved by the story of the tragic ending of Dara Shikoh, Shah Jehan's heir apparent, and read his biography, though it was not part of our course. We learned about the 'Black Hole' of Calcutta, where 'several hundred' British suffocated after being locked up in a small room by the Indian soldiers during the 'Mutiny' of 1857. In retrospect and reality, it was a gross exaggeration. The history taught to us had a decided British tilt to it.

In Geography, we learned general world geography with an emphasis on the countries of the British Commonwealth. Again, Mr. Eastwood made it interesting by bringing in color pictures from the magazine -Soviet Union, a color magazine of Soviet propaganda, to illustrate what we could only imagine. Color pictures were a rarity, for all Indian magazines and newspapers were in black and white.

I maintained my ranking in class, but now I had to share it with Maharjay. He also won the gold cross. This was awarded to the top student in the catechism exam. The first and only non-Christian to do that! Our rivalry was friendly. It was amazing that in a small combined senior class, there were three students with the same last name! The Indian tradition was that students were addressed by their last name. The classmates solved this by calling Maharajay 'Tandon' or 'Fiji' and me 'Chotey' (young) Tandan' and the teachers by calling us by our first initials, M.K. and B.N. We were inoculated with B.C.G. against tuberculosis that year.

I used to bring Baba, my younger brother, to school and back on my bike. One day for some reason, I got upset with him and, instead of giving him a ride, made him jog alongside me all the way home, which he did without any complaint. I reflected on my behavior and instantly regretted it. It was an extremely mean thing to do, no matter what the transgression. It was made especially bad by seeing his compliance without complaint to anyone. To this day, I never forgot this act of pettiness on my part and his calm behavior. I vowed never to repeat such behavior. Another anecdote comes to mind. He had just got a new pair of Bata Shoe company's 'keds' (shoes to play in). We were sitting on our lawn, and he was trying them out when I remarked that he had to be careful and keep them clean. The next thing I noticed was that he was taking a step and wiping the sole of the shoe before taking the next. It was such an innocent act of obedience! I had to explain to him what I meant. Unnoticed till then by me, he had transformed from a little terror to the sweetest and most loving child you could imagine.

I received the first installment of the scholarship I got in the eighth standard. It was customary to touch the feet of all elders and offer the first 'earnings' to your mother, which I did. Mom blessed me and asked me to keep the money. I started thinking about what to do with it. After some thinking, I decided to buy a watch. Watches were a luxury, and not many people had them, especially teenagers. They were all imported, hence expensive. The most popular were Swiss-made. There were many makes and models to choose from. West End, Genevieve, Favre Leuba, and Rolex come to mind. There were round, square, and rectangular shapes with or without a second hand. They were all wind-up ones. I visited one of the many shops recommended by someone near the booksellers market on Hospital Road. After trying on several on my thin wrist, I settled on a West End with a round dial and no 'second' hand due to my limited budget. I think it cost nearly fifty rupees, at the time a large sum. I brought it home and proudly showed it to everyone and put it on, glancing at the shiny dial every few minutes. I was proud and happy and showed it to my classmates. Watches could be worn with the dial on the outer or inner part of the wrist. I chose to wear it on the outer, the more common way. A few days later, my sister remarked that I was wearing the watch on the wrong wrist. She explained that everyone wore their watch on the left wrist. I had not given it any thought when I first put it on. After she said that, I thought about it and decided that there was no reason it could not be worn on the right. I decided to leave it on my right wrist and have worn my watches there ever since.

That year my sister Sidya Bahen got married. She had been in the biology section in the Intermediate and the bachelor's degree classes at St. John's, as my father wanted her to go to medical college. I don't think her heart was in it, and she did not do academically well, though she was otherwise very bright. She soon gave up. The sooner a girl got married after eighteen years of age or after her education, the better, was the custom. My father, like many other fathers, kept an eye for eligible and desirable Khatri boys as prospective grooms. There were many Khatri boys at St. John's. He chose one- Kamta Mehrotra, who was a student in the commerce (business) section and from a local family. The usual, making the boy and girl see each other under supervision and give their consent to their family, was gone through, and the wedding was set after the engagement ceremony. This was a great progress from before, when the to-be-married couple was told of the upcoming event, with no input from them. The engagement ceremony consisted of the bride's family sending clothing, sweets, and some money to the groom's and the groom's family sending saris and some jewelry and sweets to the bride's family.

The wedding took place at Agra, which was a first in the family, in the summer of 1953. The dowry and gifts were exhibited in our drawing room with the help of relatives, especially Rajju Bhaiya, who was pretty artistic. He was the son of my father's first cousin and was in medical college at Agra. All the gifts except jewelry were practical household goods. Steel cupboards, radio, bicycle, iron, sofa and chairs, china, woolen cloth for suiting for the groom, saris, and clothes for my sister, and more. One episode needs mentioning. At the time of the 'kanyadan' (gifting away the bride) part of the ceremony, my father refused to do so. His logic was that if I 'gift' away my daughter, I can't have her back in my house, as you can't get back what you have 'gifted' away. Despite many attempts at persuasion, he would not relent. My uncle stepped up and did that part of the ceremony. The ceremony went well otherwise. My father helped my brother–in–law to get a job as an accountant at the Auditor General's office in Gwalior, a town close by, and the couple moved there.

That year the celebration of the centennial of Indian Railways took place in Delhi. My father, his friend and neighbor Paliwal Sahib, and I went to see it. I was impressed by the old steam engines and other artifacts being shown. I loved history in any form. I also saw a demonstration of radar. I didn't quite understand its importance at the time though the word was catchy and attractive. It was also nice to see New Delhi, its wide boulevards and large buildings. We also remarked how Delhi seemed to have expanded every time we visited.

Later that winter, it was Ravi Bhaiya's turn to be married. It was to take place in Bareilly, a town in north-central U.P. The Barat (marriage party) left from Kannauj. By this time, the weddings had been reduced to two or three days, and some of the rituals had been shortened or eliminated, for families had started to split up as people became more mobile and had less time. One highlight of the event was that some of us took a short train ride to Haridwar, a small town to the north, where the river Ganga, coming down from the Himalaya Mountains, enters the plains. It is an important place of pilgrimage and is crowded in the summer. I saw the fast-flowing, crystal clear, cold water eddying against the rocks, quite a contrast to the slow-flowing darker river at Kannauj, with a few Sadhus taking a dip. Ravi Bhaiya had completed his one-year training in surgery at Gwalior and was now at Bhopal in that state's medical service.

The rest of the year went by without any major problems, and the boys in the tenth standard took their 'senior Cambridge' exam with great support from the teachers and us. I do not remember the details except that when we came back after our annual vacation, we heard that they had all passed and done well, maintaining the reputation of St. Peter's. St. George's was another school like ours across town, and we had a friendly rivalry with them, and happily, we always prevailed.

Tenth Standard

I was now in the tenth standard. Our desk assignments changed, and we moved up front as the newly arrived ninth standard boys joined us. I don't remember how many, but no more than eight or ten. We were eight. Marthins, Swing, Theophilus, MacDonald, Tandon, Tandan, Ali, and Singh. Four Anglo-Indian Christians, two Hindus, a Muslim, and a Sikh, representing the major religions of India in one small class! What were the chances of that?

The math got more advanced and difficult. In English, we had Macbeth and Thirty-nine steps. Science became more complicated, and History and Hindi became more detailed and advanced. We were a cohesive group. We got along well. There was never any rancor or disputes. The usual teenage teasing, joking, and mischief went on. I think the teachers liked us, we liked them too, and in retrospect, they were really great teachers. There were more students in the lower standards and more traffic at the start and end of school, with children being dropped off and picked up on bicycles, rickshaws, tongas, and an occasional car. The boarding students dwindled a bit as the demographics changed to less Anglo Indians and out-of-town students coming in.

That summer, I visited Ravi Bhaiya in Bhopal for a week. Bhopal was a small princely state, about four hundred miles to the south, which, for political reasons, was recognized as a class 'C' state in a complicated system of class A through class C states forming the country. Arriving by a direct overnight train, I was unimpressed by the small station and took a tonga to Ravi Bhaiya's place, who lived about two miles away with his wife, in the Police Lines, as he was the police medical officer. A wide road led to the Police Lines. The town was hilly and surrounded by low green hills, which was a pleasant surprise, coming as I was from the flat plains of North India. It was also notably cooler than Agra.

It was an old, small, congested town, surrounded by new outskirts with wide roads with gateways, two large lakes, one smaller than the other (Bara Tal and Chota Tal). It had a profusion of mosques of all shapes and sizes, as the population was mostly Muslim. I met the Superintendent of Police and had a tour of the town in his jeep. I had heard of the famous Sanchi Stupa nearby. It was an ancient Buddhist monastery building, and I decided to visit it.

I took the short passenger train ride one morning to the tiny station of Sanchi. The stupa, on a small hill a short distance away, was visible from the station. I walked over to a booth at the bottom of the hill manned by one lonely man. He seemed happy to see me and sold me the entrance ticket. I was the only tourist. We chatted for a while, and he told me that there were not many visitors; nearly all came in the winter, and most of them were foreigners. He gave me some brochures and a guidebook and advised me to visit the nearby Heliodorus pillar and the caves with Buddhist paintings in the hills nearby, if I had the time.

I climbed up the hill and surveyed the small monument with its beautiful carvings, especially the famous western gate. I sat surveying the surrounding hills and imagining the Buddhist teachers and students inhabiting the place chanting- “Budham sharanam gachchami. Dhammam saranam gacchami’ (taking refuge in the Buddha and the religion), in Pali, as I had lunch packed by Bhabhi- (sister-in-law, older brother’s wife).

Around noon time, I came down and once more consulted the lonely and bored clerk about the other attractions he had mentioned. He recommended I hire a tonga on the main road outside the station. There I hired a tonga to take me to the famous pillar. The tonga driver was an affable and voluble Muslim man. After he got acquainted with me, he told me of the hard life, the few tourists, and the lack of appreciation by people for the importance and richness of the ancient sites nearby. It was about an hour's ride, except for an occasional donkey cart or pedestrian, on the lonely road. We arrived at a cluster of mud-plastered small houses and got off. He parked the tonga under the shade of a tree, and we walked on a narrow path between the houses to a stone pillar, about 18' tall, with several areas marked with red paste. It was from the 2nd century B.C. I was happy to touch it and again fantasized a little about the time it was built. We then drove to the caves, and I admired the partially faded paintings of Buddha, people, and myths. We rode back to Sanchi station. I was filled with wonder and appreciation and enjoyed the pleasant conversation with the tonga driver. I asked him for the fare, and he said five rupees would be fine. I gladly gave him an extra half rupee for the pleasant ride and his loquacious companionship. I took the evening train back to Bhopal and excitedly related my adventure to bhaiya and bhabhi, who were glad that I enjoyed it. That was the highlight of my trip to Bhopal.

I learned from Mac that he was applying for the Joint Services Wing examination. I had no idea what that was. He explained that it was an exam for selection to the Military Academy, where you got trained for four years and were then selected to whichever military branch you could qualify for. Being competitive, I, too, decided to apply. The written exam was in Delhi a few months later. I told my father about it, and he did not seem to mind. I went to Delhi and stayed with a former student of his who was a professor at Delhi University. A few weeks later, I got a letter notifying me of my selection for the practical part of the exam to be held in Meerut, a town near Delhi. Mac was also selected. We went for the exam. It was quite an experience for me.

Arriving at the appointed place, I was met by an officer, and after some paperwork, an orderly took my luggage and led me to a large well-appointed room. He constantly addressed me as 'Sahib' (Sir). To be addressed like that by a middle-aged man was strange and flattering to a teenager. He asked me to call him if I needed anything and to leave my shoes outside at night to be polished. I was awed. I learned later that all military commissioned officers were assigned an orderly, who was like a servant cum valet, and we were being treated like officers.

There were roughly fifty of us in the group I was in. We went through short footraces, jumps, hurdle races, short speeches on topics given, short quizzes, and a psychological exam over two days. On the final morning, there was a medical exam and blood, stool, and urine tests. We were then dismissed to return home and told that the results would be sent to us in four to six- weeks. The result arrived, and I was selected with a caveat that I had partially failed the medical exam due to 'Eosinophilia' and given a date six weeks later to have that corrected and report for another medical exam. I was extremely happy and showed the letter to my father. He seemed happy too but did not say much. I had no clue what eosinophilia was. Dad consulted Dr. Mehrotra, who said it was no big deal and that he could fix it in a week or two. My grandfather (Baba) was staying with us, and when he heard of it, he told me that only people who were destitute and couldn't afford to eat joined the military, and since I was not lacking that, there was no reason for me to join the military. My dad said it was not a good idea and dropped the subject after that. Baba's reasoning was partially based on the fact that when he was young, farmers joined the military during famines to avoid starvation. I was very disappointed, but I did not and could not say anything, as the choice was never mine. Choices were made for you and not by you, and you learned to live with that. The castles in the air I had made crumbled gradually. Mac had not been selected, so we remained classmates.

It was the end of November, and the time for the final exam had arrived. The exam was to be held in the 'Hospital' building, supervised by people from outside. Nervousness and tension were in the air. We had studied hard all year, and now was the moment of truth. The examination and answer books came from Cambridge University in England and were mailed back there to be examined. Each answer book had a blotting paper in it. There was one exam each morning. In English, mercifully, there was a choice of doing some questions on grammar or writing an essay. Needless to say, I chose to write an essay. There were choices from five or six topics, and I remember two which appealed to me- 'Mondays,' and 'The advantages and disadvantages of being young.' I chose the latter. I do not remember much else, except, as usual, I was not very confident about how I did.

All of a sudden, it was over! We were happy. A weight had been lifted off our shoulders. But it also had a sadness to it. Our school days were over. The school, and the people we had become accustomed to and comfortable with, the routine, were over. We would no longer come to school and see familiar places and people! We said our goodbyes to friends and teachers. There were promises to stay in touch and tears. The teachers wished us luck and asked us to come back to visit. It was all inevitable and bittersweet.

I enjoyed time with family and friends, reading newspapers and magazines, and going to John's library in the park, awaiting the results. I had no clue what the immediate future held. I had always aspired to write and loved History and English and wondered about being a journalist. I was also fascinated with traveling. My schooling and reading had kindled a desire to travel and see the world beyond India. The dreaming part was easy and pleasant, but the reality was different, as I had no control over achieving what I wished for.

Calcutta

I do not remember how it came about, but I was to go spend some time in Calcutta with my older sister. I was excited as I had not traveled much on my own except for a visit to Bhopal. Before that, I took a short visit to Kannauj and, as usual, had a great time with my cousins. My uncle told me of his visit to Calcutta while I massaged his feet. None of it was complimentary. He said the people were different from us, the cows were the size of our goats and the bananas tiny, and the city was crowded and dirty.

I started from Agra with a steel trunk full of woolen clothes and a bundle of my mother's tasty snacks, the usual aloo-puri (potato-filled flatbread), achar (pickle), ladoo (balls of sweets), and mathri (crunchy discs of fried bread). It was a direct train, but about a twelve-hour overnight journey. I had no problem sleeping on the hard bench in the seated position in the third class. I was eager and happy to travel and see a big city despite my uncle belittling it.

I arrived about the mid-morning at a station called Howrah, a little stiff, tired, and bleary-eyed. There was the usual chaos of people getting off, luggage being hauled by coolies, and the mobile vendors on the platform. I stood and waited, a little away from the crowd, and after a little while, I saw jijaji (brother–in–law), and after touching his feet and happy greetings, we came out of the station, as he asked about my journey. We took a taxi, and on the way, I filled him in about people and news from home. I noticed that I was sweating profusely, and the wide street was noisy and crowded with rickshaws pulled by men, cars, trucks, buses, and tram (trolley) cars. The language I heard was unintelligible. I realized that I was dressed for the winter weather of north India, and it felt like our spring weather there. I took off my coat and vest. After about a half hour, we turned into a narrower street with several curves and came to a stop in front of a narrow four story building.

We went into a dark quadrangle with some sunlight filtering down from the space above. We went up a flight of stairs to his rooms. My sister was excited and happy to see me, as I was to see her. It was an old-style building with small rooms and a balcony up front. Jijaji had part of the second and third floors, and his older brother and his wife had the top floor with an open roof. The rest of the building was rented except for a few rooms on the first floor, which were his law offices. (He was a tax attorney). I had a bath, some lunch, and slept for a while, for I was more tired than I thought I was.

I was filling my sister in with the family news, answering her inquiry about the people back home, and talking with her children when Kanahi bhaiya walked in. He was my Bua's (father's sister) oldest son and a few years older than my sister. He was good-looking and jovial. My father had written to them about my visit. He promised to show me around and asked me to visit the next day. He was in the insurance business. Jijaji came home, his older brother and his wife came down, and we had some more general conversation.

The next morning my sister and I were sitting on the roof, in the sun, talking, when I heard a hawker shouting "pyara laylo, pyara laylo" ("buy love, buy love") in the street below. I was puzzled. Why would a hawker be shouting "buy love"? I asked my sister. She laughed and said that in Bengali, guava was called pyara. In Hindi pyara means love! A little later, another hawker announced, "cheena badam laylo" (buy Chinese almonds). I asked my sister what was so special about Chinese almonds. She laughed again and replied that he was selling roasted peanuts. Peanuts were Chinese almonds in Bengali. I realized that I was in for a lot of such surprises. In the afternoon, I went out for a walk to check out the area. The narrow street was called Balram De Street, and the houses were old and multistoried, with young men in their twenties hanging around outside, in small groups in passionate discussions while drinking tea and smoking. The street meandered into a larger road called

Vivekananda road. It was wide, noisy, choked with traffic, and lined by all kinds of stores. At a corner, I saw a man dressed in tatters squatting by the side of an open drain and fishing out things from it with both hands, piling them on the street and trying to pick things out of it- what, I could not tell. I was disgusted. Despite seeing poverty where I came from, I had never seen such a sight. I walked back, getting a better idea of the area. The young men were still there, animated and puffing their cigarettes and sipping tea.

The next morning Jijaji said that his clerk would show me the way and escort me to my aunt's place, which was within walking distance and not too far away. He introduced me to his clerk-Romesh Babu. He was a short skinny middle-aged man who spoke very little English and no Hindi. We started in the direction of Vivekananda road, and he led me across it, dodging chaotic traffic coming at us from both directions. We walked up two blocks. I was trying to take mental notes as I followed a step behind him. We stopped at the next intersection. He pointed to a shop and said, "Ghoray kay dokan" loudly. It was a watch repair shop, as indicated by the sign above it in English and, I presume, in Bengali. I was puzzled. Seeing the expression of non-comprehension on my face, he became more animated and repeated what he had said even louder, with his hand pointing to the shop. I remained stumped. I could not figure out what a watch repair shop had to do with a horse having two ears. ‘Ghoray kay do kan’ means ‘horse’s two ears’ in Hindi. In desperation now, he pointed to the watch on his wrist and to the shop again. I hesitated a bit, and it suddenly dawned on me! He was pointing at the watch repair shop as a landmark for me to find my way back. He had tried to speak in Hindi, and the heavy Bengali accent of the words had changed the Hindi 'ghari' (watch) to’ ghoray’ (horse) and ‘Dukan’ (shop) to ‘dokan’ (two ears). So the watch shop became a ‘horse’s two ears!’ I smiled broadly and nodded my comprehension as we made a left, and reaching Sikdar para lane, entered it and stopped outside the door of a two-story house. Romesh Babu seemed a bit relieved, and I thanked him in Hindi, as he, still slightly agitated, left.

After I rang the doorbell, a man opened the door and led me up a flight of stairs. They had been expecting me. We went through the usual inquiry about people and news from home. My aunt was a stern-looking woman with her mother’s big eyes. They had adopted my uncle’s (phupha ji) brother’s children, three girls, and a boy, in addition to having three sons and a daughter of their own. The house had the same plan as other old houses, small rooms and a corridor around a quadrangle open to the sky. Both the older sons were married. The second son, Gopal bhaiya, was in medical college, was Ravi Bhaiya’s age’ and the daughter was a few years older than me. The nieces were teenagers, and the nephew was a few years older than me. Kanhai and Gopal bhaiya were married and had their own rooms. The rooms were well-appointed. They had a device called a radiogram (a combination of a radio and an automatic record player) in their rooms. My uncle was the general manager of an insurance company. He was dark with light pockmarks on his face. My uncle and the older sons had cars.

At lunchtime, Kanhai bhaiya came home and, after lunch, took me with him. We moved through the wide but congested streets of Calcutta. I accompanied him as he called on his clients in tall modern buildings. It was all very new and fascinating to me. We did not have a car, and there were not that many in Agra, so I enjoyed the rides and seeing the large, spread-out city with so many cars. Also, elevators were a novelty. Most of his clients were non-Bengali. We came home late and had dinner and more conversation as I felt more at home. He dropped me off at my sister's around nine and said he would pick me up the next morning after breakfast. I related my activities to my sister and Jijaji. It would work out well, for Jijaji went to the courts in the morning and came home late in the evening, so had it not been for Kanhai bhaiya, I would either sit home or try to see Calcutta on my own, which would have been somewhat difficult for me.

Kanhai bhaiya showed me around Eden gardens, Ballygunge, the race course, and the outer non congested areas of the city. It was a metropolis in every sense of the word, and I was a bit awed, coming from a provincial town. I came to my sister's late again. After hearing my wide-eyed account of the things I saw, Jijaji said maybe I should stay at my Uncle's. I agreed, for I wanted to see as much as possible in my short stay, not realizing till later, in my youthful innocence, that he was a little miffed. The next morning I took some of my belongings with me when Kanhai bhaiya came to pick me up. That evening we went to Victoria memorial, a beautiful building, and had 'moori' (spicy puffed rice and raw onion bits served in a newspaper cone), being sold by hawkers. I was feeling more comfortable and confident, so the next day, I took the tram on my own and visited the New Market, a huge indoor market with each section specializing in the goods sold. I bought some souvenirs and small gifts. In the evening, I saw a huge neon sign of a cup and a kettle lit up atop a large Victorian building, advertising Lipton tea. I had never seen such a large neon sign before. I saw the famous Howrah Bridge and its huge traffic jams several times and became familiar with the word 'Jaam', meaning a traffic jam.

My father had given me the name and address of a family and asked me to pay his respects to them. They were of the same Tandon family line as us. I visited them. They lived in a huge house not far away. I was met by an 'uncle' who welcomed me eagerly, informed the ladies inside, who came to see me, and showed pleasure in seeing me. I touched the feet of everyone who looked older than me, as per tradition. He was an attorney. They offered lunch, but I made some excuses and left. I later learned that the family had supported my dad by sending him some money periodically while he was at the University, and my dad was grateful and never forgot the generosity.

Kanahi bhaiya showed me some of the famous restaurants and bought some pastries from one called Firpo's, which were delicious. One evening he invited some of his clients and their wives to a movie, about thirty of them! He and I were a little late due to traffic. It was a grand place (I don't remember the name of the movie house). The movie was 'Johnny Dark', starring Tony Curtis. We were led in by an usher with a flashlight into the dark hall. I looked to my right and saw a huge section of seats extending to the wall. At intermission, I looked around at the magnificent interior and looked to my right and saw that there was a floor-to-ceiling mirror that reflected the seats making it seem huge in dim light!

It was time to go back home. I came back to my sister's place. Jijaji did not seem very pleased, but at the time, I was too young to understand the intricacies of relationships and sensibilities. My sister did not show any sense of displeasure. I said goodbye to everyone and thanked them, and took the train back home.

I thought about my visit on the journey back. It was a novel and educational experience. I saw immense poverty and congestion, people speaking a different language, leading a faster life, and the hustle-bustle of a large city. The rickshaws were pulled manually by skinny men, mostly from the neighboring poor province of Bihar, who were also laborers. Most major Industrialists and business people were non-Bengalis. My uncle's company, Kanhai bhaiya's and Jijaji's clients, and the social circles they moved in were all non-Bengali, though they had been born and brought up there and spoke fluent Bengali. I noticed that both my uncle and Jijaji had switched their last names from Mehrotra to Khatri to try to fit in. For the first time, I felt the sense of being a 'foreigner'.

There was also extreme wealth. There was Park Street and other posh areas with gleaming cars, multi-storied buildings, shops, restaurants, and movie houses, which catered to the wealthy. Calcutta was the playground of the managers of the isolated tea plantations in the Himalayan foothills, who were mostly British. I noticed that there were many Chinese who had store-front Dental clinics. On the whole, my visit was both educational and enjoyable.

To College

I was at the John's library when I heard that the Senior Cambridge results had arrived. I rushed to school to the Principal's office, taking the shortcut right behind the library. Mr. Merriman was sitting in his office. I knocked, and he looked up, smiled broadly, and asked me to come in. "Congratulations, my boy! You passed! You made the school proud!" He said. I went in overjoyed, and he showed me the broadsheet with our results. Everyone had passed. I had all 'A's except for a 'C' (one grade lower than 'A') in math and passed with a '1st division'. The only slight disappointment was that I came second in class as Maharajay had all 'A's. Mr. Merriman shook my hand, patted my back, wished me luck in life, and asked me to stay in touch. I left his office with happy tears tinged with sadness streaming down my cheeks, as I headed home through the shortcut, glancing back at the school as it disappeared behind me. I felt happy to have kept up my grades but sad to leave a comfortable routine, people, and place to which I had become accustomed. I had no idea what the future held for me, for I had never given it any thought.

Everyone seemed happy when I told them of the results. After a few days, my father informed me that he had had me admitted to R.E.I. College in Dayalbagh, about two miles away. I was a little surprised, as everyone in the family had gone to St. John's.

I was not familiar with the college. I was in the science/biology section and was joining the last session of the first year. On the first day, I sat in a class of about forty students, with about fifteen of them girls, who sat in the front. I had never been in a class this big and never with girls. It was larger than the size of all four upper standards at St. Peter's! I did not know a soul, and no one tried to socialize. The lecture was different, and the subject, Botany, was new to me. So it started out ominously. After a few days, I was still on my own, with a few boys interacting with me during labs, and I had a feeling that I did not belong. Naresh, my neighbor, was also in that college but one year ahead of me. So that did not help. After a few weeks, I stopped going. My father found out and gave me an earful, but I told him that I would not be able to make it there. I had made up my mind that no matter what the consequences, I would not go back. After a while, he calmed down and gave up. After a few days, I heard from Sidya Bahen that I would be admitted to the second-year class at St. John's at the start of their academic year in July. I was happy about the reprieve. One day I mentioned to my father that I wanted to study in the 'Arts' section to try to become a journalist. He dismissed it outright, saying that I would end up becoming an upper division clerk in the bureaucracy somewhere.

St. John's was a large, long, and imposing red sandstone building incorporating Mughal architecture, about a mile and a half from our place. The main building was on the left, slightly set back, and below the level of the main road, the old Drummond Road, now called Mahatma Gandhi Road, as it descended from the arch over a railroad track. The college complex was on both sides of the road. On the right were the science buildings, some hostels (dormitories), and playing fields. Between the main building and the road was a hockey field and tennis and volleyball courts. A low brick wall separated the road from the college on both sides. My father took me for my interview for admission held in the imposing main hall. I was asked a few questions and advised I was accepted.

The first day was no different than at the last college. I did not know anyone, and I got curious glances from a few classmates who noticed me. I would sit in the back of the amphitheater by myself. The subjects which were compulsory were Physics, Chemistry, English, and Hindi. The only choice was between Biology and Math. It was a large class in physics, chemistry, and English and smaller in Biology as the class split into biology and math sections. I was trying to adjust to the routine and found biology challenging, as I did not have that at school and missed the first year of it. (Senior Cambridge was equivalent to the first year in college, so students from my system got admitted to the second year in college). All teachers were male and addressed as 'Sir', and the class stood up as the teacher entered. He took attendance by calling out individual's last names from a register and getting 'present Sir' as the answer. A seventy percent attendance was required in class and eighty percent in the lab. To ask a question, a student had to raise a hand and await permission, and stand when speaking to the teacher.

I was sitting in the back of the English class of Mr. David, somewhat bored, and was looking out at the street through the window when I was startled by a loud, "You there in the back! What are you smiling for?" Taken aback and unaware that I was smiling, I stood up and replied, "Oh! For nothing, Sir." "Those who smile for nothing should be in the mental asylum", Mr. David said in a sarcastic tone of voice. By now, the entire class had turned around and was gawking at me. I felt insulted and did not feel that having a smile on my face warranted mental asylum. "It has to be determined, Sir, who needs to be in the mental asylum," I replied. Mr. David turned purple, pointed toward the door, and said, "Get out of my class!" A little perplexed, I walked down the steps and out of the class into the sunshine outside. I walked over to the shade of a tree nearby, trying to fathom what had just happened. I had not intended to make a scene and had meant to imply that the act of smiling did not merit mental asylum.

Soon the class was over, and I was surrounded by my classmates. Some patted me on the back, some smiled at me and marveled at my courage to show a teacher up, and some shook my hand. I instantly became one of them. No more a stranger! Santosh Tandon, Vijay Mehra, Jitendra, and Brijveer Singh introduced themselves and accepted me into their group. I soon discovered that Vijay and I had gone to Kindergarten in his family's Tonga.

At home that afternoon, my father let me have it despite my attempt at explanation. At college, he had the reputation of being a strict disciplinarian, and that his own son had been 'insulting' to a teacher was intolerable to him. Next day I was summoned to the Principal's office, and I saw my father sitting in his chair. He was acting Principal that day. He fined me ten rupees and, knowing that I did not have that, handed me a ten rupee note to give to the office clerk. He also ordered me to tender a written apology to Mr. David.

The Hindi class had two sections. Elementary Hindi and the regular subject. I was in the elementary section as it was for students who came from non-Hindi-speaking areas and those who came from schools like mine. So the son of the professor and head of the Hindi department was in the elementary Hindi class! I was ribbed for that by my friends.

St. John's was founded in 1850 by the Christian Mission Society of England, was one of the oldest, and had the reputation of being one of the elite colleges in India. It was affiliated with Agra University. Students came to it from all over the country. There were four male and one female hostels on campus. It also had a reputation of being a more disciplined college as compared to the other three in town, for some college students were reputed to be hooligans and caused all sorts of problems. Because of my father, I was familiar with some of the professors and teachers, as some of them had often come to our house. I remember Principal Rev. Sully, a mild-mannered Englishman, who rode a bicycle. After him came Principal Mahajan and, during my time, Principal Chandi from Kerala.

The college started around ten in the morning with a general assembly of all students in the main hall, with female students on the balcony. Important announcements were made, and the Principal addressed any matters he wanted to convey. Science students went across the main road to their section, and classes started. Just outside the main gate was a crossroad. On one side was Atto's pan and tobacco shop and a fast food shop. Across the street, between it and the brick boundary wall of the science section, under a large tree, were several vendors who sold roasted unshelled peanuts in the winter, freshly roasted corn on the cob on their coal-fired brazier in the fall, bananas and guavas, and Bhalla (round potato pancake) hot off the griddle, from their pushcarts, all year round. All did a fabulous business.

I remember most of my teachers fondly. They were all good, some better than others. No matter how familiar you became with a teacher, there was a boundary of age and the Indian tradition of respect for a teacher that was not crossed. Mr. David and I became friends after my apology. He was a tall man with an eagle-like face, single, the warden (teacher in charge) of one of the hostels, and lived in it with the students. He liked to dress well, was an avid tennis player, and liked to complain of his 'tennis elbow'. His name among the students was Gudden Pyaray, which he hated, and no one dared to call him that.

Durrab Saheb, a Parsi, slightly plump, with leucoderma, was about my dad's age and taught us English. He was an excellent teacher. At one lecture, he described the beauty of the Sanchi stupa (an ancient Buddhist monument) in Madhya Pradesh and his anguish at the callous disregard of authorities about preserving ancient monuments, and that he saw some ancient relics being demolished and grinded down for road construction. I had visited Sanchi. It resonated with my sensibilities. He was also a professional photographer.

Professor Mathur taught us Physics. He had a gruff voice, was a good teacher, and would ask us questions in his inimical way, "Tandan ab tum batao" ("Tandan, now you answer"). Ram Sahab was another physics teacher, and his favorite expression was "farak farak" ("separate and distinct"), and he used it as many times as he could.

Khan Sahab was our demonstrator in physics. He was short, fair, slightly plump, middle-aged, single, and also lived in one of the hostels. He was jovial and had an eye for the ladies. It was said that he came to the college as a student and never left. St. John's became his home. He loved pan and perfumed tobacco. Bhambhani Saheb, one of the chemistry teachers, was his close friend, and they were often seen walking arm and arm with their hands in each other's coat pockets on winter evenings, headed for the pan shop. Everyone liked him.

I, like most others, had had no experience in dealing with girls except in our families and families of close friends. There was a natural attraction to them due to proximity and youth. Society, especially Hindu and Muslim, did not allow or tolerate a girl to have any relationship other than as a daughter, sister, niece, or aunt, before marriage. Things were changing now, with co-education in colleges, movies, popular movie love songs, and access to literature. But the society and the older generation had not adjusted, or they did not know how to. An interaction between a boy and a girl as a friend, like between boys, was inconceivable, except in romantic terms. Attraction and exposure to the opposite sex were natural and common but could only be actuated in secret and with dire consequences if discovered, especially for the girls. Youth could be checked but not denied. There were some secret 'liaisons' consisting of smiles, glances, exchange of, or passing of notes, and sometimes a quick chat behind a wall or bush. A girl might 'accidentally' drop her handkerchief near a boy. Any or all of these were considered 'romance' and were a big deal. A boy or girl would get teased by friends if any attraction to the opposite sex was shown or discovered. In the classroom, there was segregation, with girls sitting up front. They also teamed up in practical classes and labs. Boys teased the girls with snide comments, practical jokes, and remarks. There was a Sikh girl who was teased with '12', as in six and six are 12 etc., for it was said (in jest), that the Sikhs went crazy at the hour of 12.

My cousin Baby (Surendra) had also joined St. John's that year in the third-year Biology section and moved in. He and Naresh became friends, being in the same year though in different colleges. Baby also played volleyball and joined the N.C.C. (national cadet core, which was an auxiliary of the military in colleges). He loved movies and film songs and studied with the radio playing music, which I found very distracting. He was a prankster.

We had to have my father's permission to go to the movies or anywhere else. Once, Naresh, Baby, and I went to the movies. The ticket was one rupee and one anna after student concession, two annas for the bicycle stand, and one anna for a paper bag of roasted-in-the-shell peanuts. Since we were always scraping for money, it was tough to come up with one and a quarter rupee. After parking our bicycles, as we headed to the ticket window, Baby said he had forgotten his money at home. Naresh was mad, and we searched our pockets and found just enough money to buy Baby's ticket, knowing full well that we would never get it back. After that, Baby had to fork up the money before we went to the movies. He would also visit Naresh and pinch a new razor blade or two. A few minutes later, we would see Naresh come looking for them as he knew the culprit was Baby! (Razor blades were expensive.)

I became close friends with Santosh, Vijay, Brijvir, and Jittay. We had a good time together. Often on Sundays, we would bicycle over to the Sadar bazaar to walk around and ogle the girls or just walk up and down, as we could not afford to go to any restaurant or buy anything.

I tried to play football (soccer); not only was I small, but the talent of a larger group at college was better than mine. I soon gave up. Football was still played bare feet with an elastic sock covering only the forefoot and ankle, called an 'anklet', or wearing canvas shoes. Football boots were too expensive. Santosh and Vijay played tennis. Santosh also played cricket and was on the college team.

Tragedy struck the family –Baua died. One afternoon my mother and Baua had gone to the nearby Hewitt Park to hear a discourse on Gita. On the way back, my mother waited to cross the road to our house as a car approached, but Baua did not and was hit. She was taken to the hospital unconscious and with multiple external injuries. She never regained consciousness though her wounds healed, and she died after about fifteen days. My mother was devastated. She blamed herself for not holding on to her. It was the first death I experienced in the family. She was in her seventies. As per custom, all males in the family had their heads shaved. Somehow Baby escaped with only a haircut. It was quite an experience going to college with a shaved head. Snide remarks were made by some classmates, but that died down when they learned of the reason for it.

In December, the Russian leaders Bulganin and Khrushchev visited India and, like all foreign VIPs, visited Agra to see the Taj Mahal. There was great publicity and excitement generated by the Indian government, and there were large crowds lining their route and banners welcoming them as they passed by in an open car. My friends and I also went to see them.

The year passed pretty rapidly, with me confiding to my friends how tough I found it to keep up in class and not being sure of how I would fare on the final exams. I had not told any of them of my standing at my school. As winter ebbed, all of us started to study hard, staying up late at night. I liked to study sitting up in bed with the mosquito net around me as the mosquitos would leave everyone else alone and make a beeline (mosquito line?) for me. Baby studied as usual with the radio on at low volume.

The exams would be a question paper each in English, Hindi, Botany, Zoology, Organic chemistry, Inorganic chemistry, and two in Physics. All answers were essay-type and had to be completed within three hours. There was one exam a day. The practical exam in the science subjects preceded the written one and was conducted by a teacher from a college in a different city, along with our professor.

The practical exam in Botany and Zoology went well. In Physics, Khan Saheb tried to help everyone. I was not happy with my Inorganic chemistry exam. I voiced my usual lack of confidence to my friends, saying that I did not do well. Each day of the exam, my mother would place a small amount of dahi-batasha (yogurt on a small piece of sugar cake) in my mouth before I left for the exam, as was done to warriors going out to battle long ago, to bring good luck. She did the same with Baby.

The written exams were held in the college hall. Sealed envelopes containing the question papers and copies (answer books) were opened by the superintendent and then given out to the examinees at their desks. The time was announced, and the exam began. Two invigilators, usually teachers, walked up and down the aisles between the rows of seats, making sure that no talking or cheating took place. Attempts at cheating did go on. These were of many kinds. Writing anticipated answers on the forearm, on pieces of paper hidden up the sleeve, or in a pocket. Some clever ones took the question paper to the bathroom and gave it to a waiting friend, and retrieved the answers on a second visit to it. Whispering among examinees also occurred, though cautiously, for being caught meant disqualification and failure. Students came prepared with an extra fountain pen as a precaution and with ink bottles. Each answer book came with a blotting paper in it. After three hours, "Time's up!" was announced, and the answer books were collected. Names were not allowed to be written anywhere. Each student had a roll number which had to be written on the front of the answer book. Marks were out of a hundred in each subject, and each question had the marks allotted to it written next to it. Passing marks were 33 and above. 33 to 44 was third class, 45 to 59 second class, 60 to 74 first class, and 75 and above, distinction. If you passed all subjects except one by a few marks, you were allowed to take a supplementary exam a few months later in that subject. The final 'division' was a total of all subjects. All exams were essay-type questions. Marking was strict in most subjects, and only the very good students attained first division or distinction. This gave a distinct advantage to math students, as their answers, if correct, added up to much higher scores than other students with essay-type answers. Therefore they had much higher numbers with the first division.

In the inorganic chemistry exam, a question worth five marks involving numbers baffled me. I was nervously pondering it when I overheard the student ahead of me whisper how to solve the same problem to the one ahead of him. I followed the instructions and got the answer (it was a number). I heard them whispering the answer to each other and had a different number than mine. I re-checked mine and found it added up correctly. I nervously whispered the correct answer to the one ahead of me. He checked, found I was right, and let the one ahead of him know. Even though I overheard how to solve the question by sheer luck and, in gratitude, helped the person ahead of me, technically it could be considered cheating, as we were not supposed to communicate.

The end of the exams was an enormous relief as if a burden was lifted off my shoulders. I had already told my friends that I didn't think I had done well and sometimes genuinely felt that I might even fail. But it was over. I spent time sleeping late, and after the intense heat of the day had passed, I went out to see friends or bicycle with them in the evenings, mostly to the Sadar bazaar. Baby was studying intensely for the P.M.T. (pre-medical test) to qualify for selection to the medical colleges in the state, at Agra and Lucknow. It was a very tough exam because there were hundreds of candidates for about two hundred seats. I had some idea that my father intended for me to go into Medicine. The results of my exam conducted by the 'Board of education for the Intermediate and High School of Uttar Pradesh' were declared at Allahabad about six weeks later and printed in a special edition of a newspaper, which was distributed by railway and bus all over the state. A few eager and resourceful people would get it by telephone as soon as the newspaper came out. (Telephones were rare). Most had to wait for the paper to arrive at their place. There was a mad rush to the newspaper dealer's place and even to the train station to get the paper and results. The results were published under the name of the place where the exam was held, followed by the roll numbers of candidates under the first, second, and third divisions. Early on the morning of the day the results came, Kalloo (Narendra), who was visiting, took off on a bicycle to the newspaper agency. I was too nervous to do that. As he was returning after seeing my results, he heard a few choice curses hurled at him from behind. It was Santosh. Santosh had first looked for his results and found it in the second division, then looked for mine in the second, then in the third, did not find it and thought that I had failed, as I had shown doubts after the exam. He glanced at the short first-division list out of curiosity, and there was my roll number! He was happy for me but mad that I had fooled him by saying I had not done well, and here I was in the first-division column! He was headed home when he mistook Kalloo for me and let him have it!

All my friends had passed too. We gathered together and celebrated, and like most evenings, we went to Sadar Bazar. Sometimes we just gathered at someone's place or went to the movies. The marks needed for the first division were 300, and I had gotten 304. I thought back. Had it not been for the question, which was worth five marks, where I had overheard the solution, I would have scored 299- a second division! I had no idea what the future held for me as it was not under my control, and I had no choice.

Baby had applied again for the PMT (pre-medical test) for selection to the two medical colleges in the state, Lucknow, and Agra. I had not. Unbeknownst to me, my father had sent applications to the newly opened medical college at Bhopal and All India Institute of Medical Sciences at Delhi, for there the selection was based on the scores at the 'Intermediate' or higher degree and was open to applicants from anywhere in the country. One day he told me that I had been selected for an interview for admission at both. Bhopal was the first. Normally it would have been a cause for celebration, but that was not what I wanted to do.

I went to Bhopal for my interview and was selected (details in a different book). The plans for the interview at A.I.M.S. were dropped, for Ravi Bhaiya was at Bhopal, and that would be a better fit. There was no input in all this from me, and none was expected. Such was the state of affairs. The elders knew better and acted accordingly, making the major decisions of one's life. There was little, if any, choice offered. It was an age-old tradition, still carried out in a changing society which let you see what independence was like but not have it. It was like the Indian movies, where a boy meets a girl, falls in love, and ultimately love triumphs, but it didn't translate into real life. Ambition could be felt, embellished, and cherished, but not gained in most cases. It was like a beautiful mirage, so tantalizingly perceived but unattainable. The dreams I had were not realized, but they did not vanish. The castles in the air I had longingly constructed crumbled, succumbing to reality, but remained deeply etched in the recesses of my mind.

That's the way it was. Now a new chapter in my life, not conceived by me, was about to begin.

Family Tree

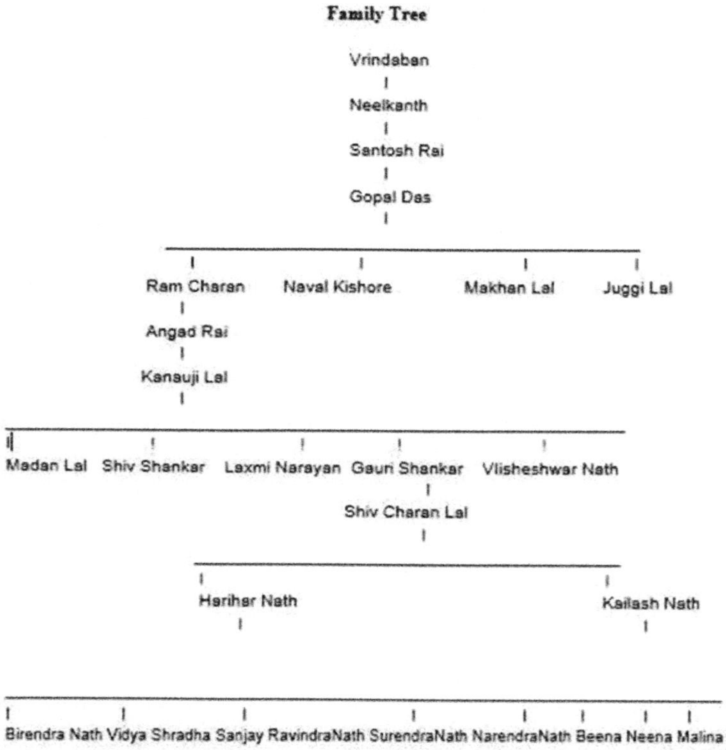
Family Tree
Vrindaban
Neelkanth
Santosh Rai
Gopal Das
Ram Charan
Naval Kishore
Makhan Lal
Juggi Lal
Angad Rai
Kanauji Lal
Madan Lal
Shiv Shankar
Laxmi Narayan
Gauri Shankar
Vlisheshwar Nath
Shiv Charan Lal
Harihar Nath
Kailash Nath
Birendra Nath
Vidya
Shradha
Sanjay
RavindraNath
SurendraNath
NarendraNath
Beena
Neena
Malina

The Thumbnail Sketch of My Generation

I would like to now introduce members of my generation of the Tandon descended from Lala Shivcharan Lal (his official name with an honorific prefix Lala), pet name Babu (Another honorific) Channulal- our grandfather- Baba

Vidya (Bidya) Bahen

Vidya, called Bidya Bahen by us, was born at Kannauj in 1928, the firstborn of my parents and of my generation. Ever since around 1936, she lived and grew up in Kannauj, with the Kannauj part of the family, while her (our) parents lived in Agra. This move, in my view, was because my Uncle's second wife, Chachi (my aunt), would have been by herself with my grandmother (Baua), with a great age difference between them. She would also provide some company in a relatively large house.

She was light-skinned, lively, exuberant, good-natured, and open. She also had a naturally loud voice. My father used to remark that she was born with a loudspeaker in her throat! I did not grow up with her and only saw her when we visited Kannauj. Also, she was ten years older and got married in 1946, and moved away. My cousin Baby was much closer to her because he grew up with her. Academically, she did a high school equivalency certificate called Vidya-vinodini to fulfill my father's desire to have the Tandon girls educated, for, before her time, it was not essential for a girl to have more than basic education.

She was well-traveled, especially to places of Hindu pilgrimages with her husband (Barey Jijaji). She was calm, considerate, and loving and had great judgment. She lived to be over ninety years, spending her last years enjoying her grandchildren, and passed away peacefully.

Shradha (Sidya) Bahen

Shradha, called Sidya Bahen, was two years younger than Vidya Bahen and was born in Agra. She had my mother's features. I think she was my father's favorite child. She grew up in Agra and went to Murailal Khatri school and then to St. John's College. She got married before she could finish her B.Sc. I think my father had also intended for her to go to medical college, but that did not materialize. What she did not achieve academically, she made up in other aspects of life. She was talented, practical, bright, and frank, made friends easily, and was not overly religious. Even after marriage, she really never left the family, as Gwalior, where she lived, was less than a hundred miles away, and her husband's family was from Agra, so she was back at home often, especially during major festivals.

She stayed in London for some time when my brother-in-law (Kamta jija) was posted there, while my older nephews stayed at home at our place and kept up the family tradition of attending St. John's College. She raised one of her grandsons from infancy in her middle age when one of her daughter-in-law died postpartum.

Ravi Bhaiya

Ravi Bhaiya was my uncle's oldest son, born in Agra and about a year or so younger than Sidya Bahen. He was short and had his mother's (who died when he was just five years old) good looks. He was quiet and liked by everybody. Baua (our grandmother) always kept an eye on the way he was treated by others. This was never a problem because everyone was nice to him. He had no 'nick' or 'pet' name, except my aunt from Calcutta called him 'Lummy' (short for lomari or fox), which he disliked. No one else called him that. He was smart, good at cricket, and always dressed well. He joined Agra Medical College in 1947, and I grew up with him during my formative years and idolized him. He had a motorcycle when he was in his fourth year of medical college, and I took many rides with him. Having a motorcycle was a big deal then. My uncle very much wanted him to come and practice with him at Kannauj, but he went to Bhopal to work in the state medical services there. He came back to Agra with his wife for a year to get his degree in Radiology while I was at Bhopal medical college. I lived with him in my first year there. Everyone there knew me as his younger brother, so I had to try to be on the straight and narrow for the six and a half-years I was there. He was a heavy smoker and smoked a strong brand called Charminar, and I occasionally pilfered a few from his packet when I went to visit him on Sundays. He was well-liked by the higher authorities, made steady progress in his career, and retired from its top position as Director General of Medical & Health Services of the state of M.P. (Madhya Pradesh). I loved and respected him.

Surendra (Baby)

Baby was my uncle's second son, also born at Agra, and the most colorful member of the family of my generation. He was tall, fair, good-looking, and four months younger than me. He was the favorite grandson of Baba (grandpa), who also disciplined him the most. He was also my aunt's unstated favorite child. There was not one person that I knew who did not like him. He loved good food, especially fast food (chat) of any kind, rich and spicy chicken curry, and all kinds of sweets, desserts, and ice cream. In short, he loved to eat good and rich food. Strangely, he disliked fruits of any kind intensely. He made friends easily and loved practical jokes. He was crazy about movies and film music. He was good at kite flying. We had a wonderful time together when I visited Kannauj during summer vacation.

In 1955 he came to Agra, occupying the room Ravi Bhaiya had lived in, and my father admitted him to St. John's College in the B.Sc. course in preparation for possible entry to medical college. That did not work out. He then opted to do his Masters in zoology. But due to some enmity with my father, the professor of zoology at St. John's did not select him. My father got him admitted to Agra College. After completing his master's degree, he returned to Kannauj and started teaching Biology at the local Intermediate College.

Baray (older), Jijaji (Vidya Bahen's husband), and Baby got along extremely well, for they had a lot in common. They both liked rich food and movies. Whenever Jijaji visited Agra, the two would be gone for hours to their favorite chat wallas (Chat vendors) in the inner city or to a movie. The classic example was that Jijaji's daughter Manju was being married from our home in Agra, and Jijaji was needed for some ceremony and was nowhere to be found. He and Baby had gone to see a movie!

After getting his M.Sc. in zoology he started teaching at the college at Kannauj. Every couple of weeks or so, Baby would go to Kanpur (a large city 50 miles away) to pick up things he wanted that were not available in Kannauj and to eat chicken at his favorite non-vegetarian restaurant. A proposal of marriage for Nina (uncle's second daughter) to Vishnu, a medical student at Lucknow, was in progress. Vishnu was visiting Kanpur, so my uncle dispatched Baby to meet with him and check him out. Baby did that, and to entertain him, took him to his favorite restaurant and ordered chicken curry. He had presumed that a modern young man in medical college would definitely be a non-vegetarian and wanted to impress him. Much to his chagrin, he found out that Vishnu did not eat meat and was from a very strict vegetarian family that did not even eat garlic and onion! My uncle, needless to say, was not thrilled.

Being on a teacher's salary, which was not all that much, he tried to supplement his income by doing business on the side. He tried selling fertilizer. That did not work out. He tried selling units that produced electric power from cow dung (gobar gas). That, too, did not succeed, continuing the Tandon family tradition of not being lucky in business. These were the two I know of. But he was never bitter about it and shrugged it off with his usual good humor. He was a popular teacher and a respected member and leader of the Khatri community and organized many of its events at Kannauj. He punctuated nearly all of his speech with two pet cuss words which are unprintable. But nobody took offense as they knew that was the way he spoke.

His practical jokes were amazing. One time Bina's husband Ram insisted on going back to Kanpur (his home) from Kannauj, despite requests by the family to stay another day or two. The usual travel was by bus from the depot near the railway station. Baby went with him to drop him off. At the ticket window, the teller was one of Baby's ex-students. Baby silently signaled him from behind Ram not to sell him a ticket. When Ram asked for a ticket he was told that there were no more tickets available for Kanpur. Ram was surprised and angry. He argued, yelled, and threatened, to no avail. He finally gave up and came back home with Baby!

Another joke involved Sharmaji, who lived next door in Kannauj and was a traveling insurance salesman. There was an outbreak of plague at a place in south India, and people coming from the area were quarantined under penalty of law. Sharmaji had just returned from a trip nowhere near it. Baby and Lalaji (an accomplice) anonymously called the police and reported that Sharmaji had come from the plague area. Police constables showed up and, despite denials, escorted him to the police station to prove that he had not visited the area. Sharmaji was released after giving proof. He found out who was behind this and did not forgive the perpetrators for months.

Baby's wife, Suman, who was from Kanpur, had a master's degree in English. Having her teach at the local women's school was considered but rejected by the family. They went on to have three beautiful girls, and Baby was teased about producing only girls. A National Emergency was declared in India by Indira Gandhi, under which there would be a penalty of loss of promotion and salary increase for men who had multiple children and who failed to have a vasectomy. They had to submit proof of vasectomy to authorities. Baby was squeamish about any personal discomfort, much less having to have surgery. Besides, he only had girls. Somehow, Kallu (his younger brother), who was practicing law in Kannauj, managed to get him the required proof of vasectomy.

The Emergency was over, and a few years later, Baby and Suman tried one more time. At the time of delivery at the local Obstetrical facility, he was informed that it was another girl! Slightly disappointed, he turned around to leave when the midwife exclaimed, "Wait! There's another one!" Fifteen minutes later, Baby was the proud father of a bouncing boy! He was blessed with twins! Years later, he was sometimes teased by his friends about his 'failed' vasectomy!

Barely after the age of forty, he had a heart attack. He was overweight, sedentary, and unrestricted in his diet. He tried watching his diet, unsuccessfully. Not even fifty, he had a massive heart attack and passed away. Everyone was devastated. We had grown up together, and even though I had moved to the States, when I visited every two years, nothing had changed between us. He would unburden his soul to me, and we would joke around just as we did when we were kids growing up. It was a great personal loss to me.

Narendra (Kallu)

Kallu was my uncle's third son, about two years younger than Baby, born in Kannauj. I don't know how he got that nickname (dark), for he was not dark. Maybe he was only a shade darker than Baby. He grew up with Baby and me. Being younger, he was at times teased and picked upon by us, but he always held his own. What he lacked academically, he made up by being smart and observant. I remember he gave evidence in a court case at Fatehgarh (the district court) about some case involving a bank at Kannauj when he was only about seven or eight years old. It was hard for him to grow up in the shadow of a brother who was the blue-eyed child of the family- but he showed no sign of resentment. When he finished his 'Intermediate' in arts section at the Intermediate- College in Kannauj, my Uncle thought of starting him in some business, one of which was opening a factory to manufacture sunglasses. My father wanted him to have higher education. My father, who was an advocate for higher education, prevailed. So Kallu followed the Tandon boy's tradition to come to Agra and join St. John's. My father had him admitted to the commerce section for his B.Com.

Unlike Baby and me, Kallu was not as prone to pranks and had more than twice the worldly smarts than Baby, and I combined. He was not overly demonstrative and knew how to deal with people and situations appropriately. This is my view in retrospect.

So when Baby left after completing his Masters, and I was still at Bhopal, Kallu was at Agra. My father had him admitted to Law college at Agra College after he finished his B. Com. I think my father, who could not finish his Law degree (due to financial reasons), wanted his nephew to achieve what he could not.

After I left for Bhopal, I became a stranger to many people who dealt with the family at Agra. Baby and Kallu were Prof. Tandon's sons for those who did not know the family well. One episode would illustrate that. One morning,

I was sitting reading the newspaper on the front verandah of the house while visiting Agra for a few weeks during the summer break. A man came in and asked me if Tandon saheb (my father) was in. I told him that he had gone out. He then asked whether his son was in. For a moment, perplexed, I realized he meant Kallu! I smiled and went in and got Kallu. I had become an outsider!

After getting his law degree and a few years of apprenticeship with a lawyer, who was a family friend, at Fatehgarh, Kallu started his own practice at Kannauj. In due course, he became a successful and famous lawyer in the district, practicing criminal law.

Bina

Bina, my uncle's oldest daughter, was Kannauj born and about two years younger than Kallu. She was nice looking. I have already mentioned how she was quiet and 'different' and the reincarnation episode earlier. She became very close to two of her female teachers, who were single, and taught at the girl's Intermediate- College, and rented the house my uncle had built near Chachchi's place. She spent most of her time there. After she completed her Intermediate studies, she was married to Ram, who owned a business, and lived in Kanpur, not far off.

Nina

Nina, also born in Kannauj, was about two years younger than Bina. She was her sister's opposite. Also nice looking, but boisterous, bold, and very sociable. When she was a child, she had some sort of digestive problem and frequently came to Agra, for she was under the care of a pediatrician there. As mentioned earlier, Baba (Sanjay), at times, terrorized her. She completed her bachelor's degree at the local college, which by now had become a 'degree' college (undergraduate). She was married to Vishnu, who had just graduated from medical college in Lucknow, and moved to his place in Allahabad. They later went to England for a few years and stayed with Sidya Bahen, as Kamta jijaji was posted at the Accountant General of India's office in London. Vishnu and Nina later moved to the U.S., where I had been for a few years. So there was still family togetherness!

Sanjay (Baba)

Baba was eight years younger than me. He was born in Kannauj. He was fair and slightly plump, adorable, and somewhat of a pet in the family, for the rest of us were much older. Our father had calmed down somewhat, so he grew up without the fear of our father's disciplinarian strict phase of life. As mentioned earlier, he was a mischievous child with a touch of Tandon stubbornness. As he grew up, he changed. He changed into the most kind-hearted, obedient, selfless boy. He was also admitted to St. Peter's, and while I was still there, I took him to school on my bicycle. I wish I had paid more attention to him, for the difference in age, the self-centeredness of my teenage years, and my moving to Bhopal at age eighteen deprived me of growing up with him and also with the family. I became someone slightly distant, who visited during the summer for a few weeks. Soon after my medical education, I moved even further away. So I still regret not growing up with him. To me, he is the personification of an ideal brother who does not have a mean bone in his body and is loving, unselfish, kind, and forgiving. I think he inherited and monopolized all of our mother's qualities. I am slightly envious of that. I might be slightly biased, being his brother, but in this case, I don't regret this shortcoming. He kept up the tradition of attending St. John's and then went to Agra Medical College, specializing in Internal Medicine, and started a private practice.

His practice initially was mostly gratis, for he would not charge anyone who knew my father, which was nearly everyone! It gradually grew as word of mouth of his skill, honesty, spread. He developed a large reputable practice among rural folk around Agra at the time when kickbacks, lack of honesty, greed, and such traits were common in medical practice. His stellar reputation was echoed to me by friends and relatives whenever I visited Agra. He was married to Asha, an Ob-Gyn specialist. His failings, as I see it, are that he is too trusting and disorganized, which he shares with me. Needless to say, anyone would be proud to have a brother like that. You may say I am slightly biased. You bet I am. He is my brother!

Malina (Muniya)

Muniya was the youngest of us all. She was Uncle's youngest daughter and last child. Many years younger than Baba and Neena. She was born in Agra and was a big baby, around nine pounds, a rarity in Indian newborns at the time. She was fair and plump and had large eyes. She grew up to be my Uncle's favorite and, being the youngest, was spoiled by all of us. She was boisterous and bubbly and quick-witted with a sweet temperament. She got her education in Kannauj and got married to a different Ram from the north-east part of U.P.

This is a thumbnail account of the offspring of the Tandons of Kannauj-Agra. The difference in age between the oldest and youngest is over thirty years.

I sincerely hope that the reader got a glimpse of the past through my story- a past long gone, nearly erased and forgotten , even though it was- Not so long ago.

Made in the USA
Middletown, DE
24 January 2024

48095231R00170